GROUNDED IN NATURE

GROUNDED IN NATURE

DISCOVER THE HEALING POWER OF NATURE
WITH FOREST BATHING, EARTHING AND
GROUNDING (2-IN-1 COLLECTION)

HEALING POWER OF NATURE

NAOMI ROHAN

Teilingen
PRESS

To the whispering trees, the ancient stones, and the endless sky—may this book be a tribute to your unspoken wisdom.

To those who walk among you, seeking solace and connection, may they find their way back to your open arms. This is for the wanderers and the wonderers, for the hearts yearning to be grounded in the beauty of nature.

To forget how to dig the earth and to tend the soil is to forget ourselves.

— MAHATMA GANDHI

CONTENTS

FREE EBOOK BY NAOMI ROHAN: Nurtured by Nature

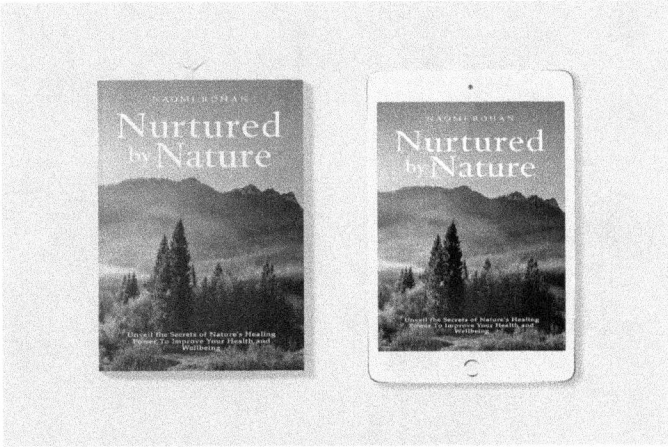

$9.99 FREE EBOOK

Scan the QR code below to download your free copy of Nurtured by Nature:

Or visit:

https://teilingenpress.wixsite.com/home/naomi-rohan

INTRODUCTION

Welcome, dear reader, to a sanctuary bound in pages, a verdant journey through the whispers of leaves and the ancient wisdom of the Earth. "Grounded in Nature" is not merely a book; it is a call to return to the roots of our existence, a two-part collection that cradles your soul in the nurturing arms of the natural world.

In today's society, where the digital hum and concrete sprawl often drown out the rustling of leaves and the softness of soil, this book is a reminder of the tranquility that awaits in the embrace of the natural world.

This collection serves as a gentle reprieve, offering you a chance to slow down, breathe deeply, and nourish your soul with the timeless wisdom of the Earth. It is a guide back to balance and harmony through the simple act of stepping outside and being present in nature's bounty.

"Grounded in Nature" aims to rekindle your bond with the outdoors and inspire a reawakening of the joys and healing properties found beyond our four walls. Through the immersive experiences of forest bathing and earthing, the book seeks to transform your life, encouraging a lifestyle that prioritizes your relationship with the natural world.

In "The Power of Forest Bathing," you are invited to wander beneath the emerald canopy, where dappled sunlight dances upon the forest floor.

Here, you will be led along the path of Shinrin-Yoku, the sacred art of forest bathing. You learn to listen to the forest's serene symphony and breathe in harmony with the rustling leaves.

"Earthing Essentials" unfurls like the rich, dark Earth beneath your bare feet, grounding you in the primordial connection we share with our planet. You are invited to step into a world where every grain of soil hums with life, where the heartbeat of the Earth resonates with your own. You will unearth the land's forgotten language, rediscovering Mother Earth's healing embrace.

"Grounded in Nature" is a companion for those who yearn to reconnect with the natural world, a guide for the seekers of tranquility, and a balm for the soul. It is a journey towards a more mindful, healthier existence, where each step on the Earth and each breath of forest air brings us closer to our truest selves and the planet that sustains us.

Embrace this journey, and let the whispers of the forest and the song of the Earth resonate within you. Turn the page and take the first step to discover the transformative power of the natural world.

THE POWER OF FOREST BATHING

A COMPREHENSIVE GUIDE TO SHINRIN-YOKU, THE JAPANESE PRACTICE OF HEALING AND MINDFULNESS IN NATURE

EMBRACING THE FOREST'S EMBRACE

In the calm stillness of the dawn, when the world is yet to stir from its slumber, the forest extends a whispered invitation. It is a call as ancient as the earth itself, a gentle beckoning that echoes through the rustling leaves and the murmuring brooks. It is an invitation to step away from the clamor of our bustling lives, leave behind the concrete jungles we inhabit, and immerse ourselves in nature's tranquil embrace.

In its timeless wisdom, the forest invites us to partake in a journey of rejuvenation and self-discovery. It invites us to tread softly upon its moss-carpeted floor, to breathe in the crisp, clean air infused with the scent of pine and damp earth, to listen to the symphony of bird songs and rustling leaves, and to let our gaze wander over the myriad shades of green that paint its vast canvas.

This whispered invitation is not merely a call to explore the physical realm of the forest. It is an invitation to delve into the depths of our being, reconnect with our roots, and rediscover the profound peace within us. It is an invitation to experience 'forest bathing,' a practice that has the power to heal, soothe, and transform.

As you turn the pages of this book, you will find yourself walking along the forest's winding paths, feeling the cool shade of its towering trees and basking in the dappled sunlight that filters through its dense canopy. You will learn to listen to the forest's whispered invitation and to respond to it with an open heart and a tranquil mind. You will learn to embrace the forest's embrace, and in doing so, you will embark on a journey that will lead you to a place of serenity, balance, and profound inner peace.

The Enchanting Dance of Light and Shadow

As you step into the forest, the world outside begins to fade, replaced by a symphony of sounds that is the forest's own. The rustling leaves, the whispering wind, and the distant call of a bird all merge into a harmonious melody that seems to resonate with your soul. But it is not just the sounds that captivate you. It is the enchanting dance of light and shadow that truly draws you in.

Imagine standing at the edge of a forest at dawn, the world still hushed in the soft embrace of twilight. As the first rays of the sun pierce the veil of darkness, they illuminate the forest in a breathtaking spectacle. The light filters through the canopy, casting dappled shadows that dance and sway with the gentle rustling of the leaves. It's a mesmerizing ballet of light and shadow, a spectacle that changes with each passing moment, each shifting leaf, each fluttering bird.

This dance is not merely a visual feast. It is an invitation, a beckoning from the forest itself. It invites you to step into its verdant heart, lose yourself in its tranquil depths, and become one with its rhythmic pulse. It is an invitation to experience forest bathing, immerse yourself in the forest's embrace, let its serene beauty wash over you, and rejuvenate your spirit.

You feel a sense of peace as you watch the enchanting dance of light and shadow. With its noise and chaos, the world outside seems distant, almost unreal. All that exists is the forest, its soothing rhythm, and its gentle whisper that seems to say, "Come, step into my heart. Let me show you a world of tranquility and beauty where you can find your rhythm and peace."

This is the magic of forest bathing. It is not just about walking in a forest. It is about immersing yourself in its embrace, letting its tranquility seep into your soul, and finding a sense of peace and rejuvenation that is as enchanting as the dance of light and shadow. It is about embracing the forest's embrace, about becoming one with its verdant heart. This book is your guide on this journey, a pathway to serenity that begins with the enchanting dance of light and shadow.

A Pathway to Serenity: Your Journey Begins Here

There lies a pathway to serenity in the gentle rustle of leaves, in the soft murmur of a brook, in the hushed whispers of the wind. This book, dear reader, is your guide to discovering that path, your compass to navigate the verdant labyrinth of tranquility that is forest bathing.

The purpose of this book is not merely to introduce you to the concept of forest bathing but to invite you into a world where the boundaries between self and nature blur, where the heart beats in rhythm with the earth's pulse. It is a journey of self-discovery, of finding peace in the embrace of the forest, of learning to listen to the silent songs of nature.

The goals of this book are manifold. It aims to guide you, step by step, into the heart of the forest, to teach you to see not just with your eyes but with your soul. It seeks to help you find a sanctuary amidst the trees, where you can shed the weight of the world and clothe yourself in tranquility. It aspires to show you how to tap into nature's healing power, bathe in the forest's refreshing energy, and rejuvenate your spirit in the cool, green shade of the woods.

This book is your journey, which begins here, in the embrace of the forest. It is a journey that will take you deep into the heart of nature, where you will find serenity and a deeper understanding of yourself and your place in the world. It is a journey that will change you and leave you refreshed, revitalized, and renewed.

So, dear reader, take a deep breath. Feel the cool, fresh air fills your lungs, taste the sweetness of the forest on your tongue. Listen to the forest's whispered invitation. Your journey begins here. Welcome to the pathway to serenity. Welcome to the world of forest bathing.

A Glimpse into the Verdant Heart of the Forest

As we embark on this journey together, we will delve into the verdant heart of the forest, where tranquility reigns, and the hustle and bustle of the world fades into a distant murmur. This book is not merely a guide but a companion, a gentle hand leading you into the embrace of the forest, where you will learn to commune with nature in a way that rejuvenates your spirit and soothes your soul.

We will begin by exploring the concept of forest bathing, a practice that originated in Japan, known as Shinrin-Yoku. This is not a physical bath but rather an immersion of the senses, a bathing in the forest's atmosphere. We will delve into the science behind it, understanding how this simple act of being in nature can profoundly affect our health and well-being.

From there, we will journey through the seasons, experiencing the forest in its many moods. We will learn to appreciate the delicate lacework of frost on a winter's morning, the vibrant explosion of spring blossoms, the dappled sunlight of a summer's day, and the fiery palette of autumn leaves. Each season brings unique gifts; we will learn to receive them with open hearts.

We will also explore the forest at different times of day, from dawn's peaceful stillness to twilight's mysterious depths. We will learn to listen to the forest's symphony, the rustle of leaves, the song of birds, the whisper of the wind. We will learn to see not just with our eyes but with our hearts, discovering the hidden beauty that lies beneath the surface.

Finally, we will learn practical techniques for forest bathing, from mindful walking to deep breathing exercises. These techniques will help you to fully immerse yourself in the forest's embrace, allowing you to tap into its healing power.

This journey is not about reaching a destination but about savoring the journey itself. It is about learning to slow down, be present, and connect with the natural world in a way that nourishes our spirit. So, let us step into the verdant heart of the forest and let its soothing whispers guide us on our path to serenity.

1

THE ORIGIN AND HISTORY OF FOREST BATHING

I n the tranquility of the dawn, when the world is still half-asleep, the forest awakens. The leaves rustle gently, whispering secrets to the wind. The crisp and fresh air carries the scent of damp earth and the subtle perfume of wildflowers. In its serene majesty, the forest invites you to step into its embrace, lose yourself in its verdant labyrinth, and find solace in its tranquil bosom. This is the essence of forest bathing, a practice as old as the forest itself yet as refreshing as the morning dew.

Forest bathing, or Shinrin-Yoku as it is known in Japan, is not merely a walk in the woods. It is a mindful immersion in the forest atmosphere, a deliberate act of connecting with nature on a deep, sensory level. It is about allowing the forest to seep into your being, to cleanse your mind, and to rejuvenate your spirit.

The genesis of forest bathing is as timeless as the forest itself. It is rooted in the primal relationship between humans and nature, nurtured by countless generations across diverse cultures and vast landscapes. It is a relationship that has evolved, adapted, and flourished, much like the forest itself.

The concept of forest bathing is not a new one. It is an ancient practice, a forgotten wisdom that has been rediscovered in our modern world.

It is a testament to the enduring allure of the forest, a testament to the healing power of nature.

The forest has always been a sanctuary, a place of refuge and renewal. It has been a source of inspiration, insight, strength, and serenity. It has been a teacher, a healer, a guide. It has been a companion, a confidant, a friend.

In its infinite wisdom, the forest has always known the secret to a balanced and harmonious life. It has always known the art of being, the art of living, the art of forest bathing. And now, it invites us to partake in this ancient wisdom, to embark on a journey of self-discovery and self-healing, to immerse ourselves in the tranquil beauty of the forest, and to bathe in its restorative embrace.

As we delve deeper into the origins and history of forest bathing, we will explore its ancient roots, Japanese influence, scientific validation, global spread, and modern adaptations. We will journey through time and space, through cultures and continents, through science and spirituality. We will journey into the heart of the forest, into the heart of forest bathing. And in doing so, we will journey into the heart of ourselves.

Ancient Roots: Forest Bathing in Early Cultures

In the hushed whispers of the past, where time was measured by the sun's journey across the sky and the changing of the seasons, our ancestors found solace and sustenance in the embrace of the forest. Though not named as such, the concept of forest bathing was deeply ingrained in their lives. It was a time when humanity was intricately woven into the fabric of nature when the forest was not just a resource but a sanctuary, a healer, and a teacher.

The ancient cultures, from the Celts of Europe to the indigenous tribes of the Americas, from the sages of India to the shamans of Siberia, all revered the forest. They recognized its power, its wisdom, and its ability to heal. They bathed in its beauty, sounds, scents, and silence, absorbing its essence into their very being. This was their form of forest bathing, a practice born out of necessity and reverence and as natural as breathing.

In these early cultures, the forest was a sacred space. It was a place of worship, a place of learning, a place of healing. The Celts, for instance, believed in the spiritual presence of trees, each species possessing unique wisdom and energy. They would retreat into the forest for meditation, healing, and guidance. The indigenous tribes of the Americas, too, held a deep respect for the forest. They saw it as a living entity, a provider, a protector. They would immerse themselves in its depths, seeking wisdom, peace, and connection.

In the East, the sages of ancient India found enlightenment under the Bodhi tree, while the monks of China sought solace in the bamboo groves. The forest was their sanctuary, source of inspiration, and pathway to spiritual awakening. They bathed in the forest's tranquility, energy, wisdom, absorbing essence, spirit, and life force.

Though varied in their rituals and beliefs, these ancient practices shared a common thread - the profound understanding of the healing power of the forest. They recognized that the forest was more than just a collection of trees. It was a living, breathing entity, a source of life, a source of healing, a source of wisdom. They understood that by immersing themselves in the forest and bathing in its beauty, energy, and silence, they could find peace and healing and rediscover themselves.

As we journey through history, we find that the essence of forest bathing has remained unchanged. It is a practice that transcends cultures and time. It is a practice that speaks to the very core of our being, reminds us of our deep-rooted connection with nature, and invites us to return to our origins.

The Japanese Influence: Shinrin-Yoku

In the heart of the Land of the Rising Sun, a practice was born that would soon ripple out across the globe, touching lives with its gentle, healing touch. This practice, known as Shinrin-Yoku, or forest bathing, is a cornerstone of Japanese culture and has profoundly influenced the world's understanding and appreciation of nature's therapeutic potential.

Shinrin-Yoku, when translated, means 'taking in the forest atmosphere' or 'forest bathing.' It was developed in Japan during the

1980s to respond to the increasing stress and health issues associated with urban living. The Japanese government, recognizing the need for a healthier, more balanced lifestyle, introduced Shinrin-Yoku as a form of ecotherapy, encouraging citizens to immerse themselves in the tranquil beauty of the country's lush forests.

The practice is deceptively simple yet profoundly impactful. It involves walking slowly, almost meditatively, through a forested area, breathing deeply, and allowing the senses to fully engage with the surrounding nature. The aim is not to reach a destination but to soak in the journey, to bathe in the forest's atmosphere, and to emerge rejuvenated and at peace.

The impact of Shinrin-Yoku on Japanese society was transformative. It not only improved physical health but also fostered a deeper connection with nature, promoting mental and emotional well-being. The practice became a bridge, linking the modern, fast-paced world with the timeless wisdom and tranquility of the forest.

The influence of Shinrin-Yoku did not stop at Japan's borders. The practice resonated with people worldwide, leading to a global renaissance of forest bathing. Different cultures have embraced the Japanese concept of Shinrin-Yoku, each adding unique interpretations and adaptations, yet united by the shared understanding of the forest's healing power.

The impact of Shinrin-Yoku is a testament to the universal human need for connection with nature. It serves as a reminder that amidst the hustle and bustle of modern life, the forest remains a sanctuary, a place of tranquility and rejuvenation, waiting to welcome us into its soothing embrace.

The Science Behind Forest Bathing

In the stillness of the forest, where the air is filled with the scent of pine and the rustling of leaves, a profound sense of healing transcends the physical realm. This is the essence of forest bathing, a practice deeply rooted in various cultures for centuries. But what is the science behind this seemingly mystical experience? Let us delve into the historical perspective of the science behind forest bathing.

The scientific exploration of forest bathing began in earnest in the 1980s in Japan, where the practice is known as Shinrin-Yoku. The Japanese government, recognizing the potential health benefits of spending time in nature, initiated a series of studies investigating the physiological effects of forest bathing. The results were nothing short of remarkable.

Researchers discovered that immersion in the forest environment could reduce blood pressure, lower cortisol levels, and improve concentration and memory. They also found that forest bathing could boost the immune system by increasing the activity of natural killer cells, a type of white blood cell that fights off viruses and cancer.

The key to these benefits, they found, lies in the natural compounds released by trees, known as phytoncides. These organic compounds, which trees emit to protect themselves from insects and decay, significantly impact human health. When inhaled, phytoncides have been shown to enhance human immune function and reduce stress hormones.

As the scientific understanding of forest bathing deepened, the practice began to gain recognition beyond Japan. Researchers worldwide started to explore nature's therapeutic effects, leading to the emergence of a new field of study known as ecotherapy.

In the 21st century, the science of forest bathing continues to evolve. Modern studies are exploring the impact of forest bathing on mental health, with promising results indicating that time spent in nature can alleviate symptoms of depression and anxiety.

The science behind forest bathing, while still a growing field, offers a compelling testament to the healing power of nature. It is a gentle reminder that the forest remains a sanctuary of tranquility and wellness in our increasingly urbanized and digital world. As we continue to explore the depths of the forest's healing potential, we are also rediscovering our innate connection to the natural world. This connection can rejuvenate our bodies, refresh our minds, and restore our spirits.

Forest Bathing Across Continents

As the sun began to rise over the horizon, painting the sky with hues of pink and orange, the concept of forest bathing, too, began to awaken and stretch its roots beyond the borders of Japan. The world was about to experience a gentle revolution, a quiet transformation that would change how we perceive and interact with nature.

The 1980s marked the beginning of this global journey. The whispers of the forest began to echo in the hearts of people across continents, from the lush greenery of Europe to the vast wilderness of North America, from the dense jungles of South America to the unique biodiversity of Australia. The concept of forest bathing was no longer confined to the Land of the Rising Sun; it was now a global phenomenon, a universal call to return to nature.

In Europe, the idea of forest bathing resonated deeply with the people. With its rich history and diverse landscapes, the continent embraced the practice with open arms. The lush forests of Scandinavia, the enchanting woods of Germany, and the tranquil groves of the United Kingdom all became sanctuaries for those seeking solace and healing in nature. Forest bathing clubs began to sprout, offering guided walks and promoting the benefits of this mindful practice.

Across the Atlantic, North America, too, was captivated by the allure of forest bathing. The vast wilderness of Canada and the United States, with their towering pines, majestic oaks, and serene lakes, provided the perfect backdrop for the practice. The concept was introduced in various wellness programs, retreats, and corporate environments, encouraging people to disconnect from their hectic lives and reconnect with nature.

In South America, forest bathing found a unique expression. The indigenous communities, with their deep-rooted connection to the land, integrated the practice into their daily lives, blending it seamlessly with their ancient traditions. With its unparalleled biodiversity, the Amazon rainforest became a haven for forest bathers, offering an immersive experience like no other.

Down under in Australia, the practice took on a different hue. The continent's unique flora and fauna added a distinct flavor to forest bathing. The eucalyptus forests, with their soothing aroma and the melodious calls of native birds, created a healing and rejuvenating environment.

As we trace the forest bathing journey across continents, we see a common thread - a universal longing for a deeper connection with nature. Despite our diverse cultures and landscapes, we are all drawn to the tranquility of the forest, the gentle whisper of the leaves, and the soothing rhythm of nature's heartbeat. This global spread of forest bathing is a testament to our shared love for nature, a reminder of our inherent need to be in harmony with the world.

Forest Bathing in the 21st Century

As the dawn of the 21st century broke, the world was in the throes of a technological revolution. The rapid pace of life, the constant connectivity, and the ceaseless hum of digital devices began to take a toll on the collective human spirit. Amidst this whirlwind of progress, an ancient practice began to re-emerge, offering a soothing balm to the frazzled nerves of modern society. This practice was forest bathing, a concept that had its roots in the tranquil woods and serene landscapes of our ancestors.

In the 21st century, forest bathing has been adapted and embraced in a myriad of ways across the globe. It has transcended cultural boundaries and been integrated into modern life's fabric, offering a gentle reminder of our inherent connection to the natural world.

In urban environments, where concrete jungles often replace green forests, city dwellers have found innovative ways to engage in forest bathing. Urban parks and green spaces have become sanctuaries, offering a slice of nature amidst the steel and glass structures. These spaces, though smaller and more contained than sprawling forests, still allow individuals to immerse themselves in nature, breathe deeply, and find a moment of tranquility in the chaos of city life.

In healthcare, forest bathing has been recognized for its therapeutic benefits. Medical professionals and therapists have begun incorporating forest bathing into treatment plans, acknowledging the healing power of nature. Hospitals and healthcare facilities have started to design healing gardens, spaces where patients can engage in forest bathing, promoting recovery and well-being.

In education, schools and universities have started to recognize the value of forest bathing. Outdoor classrooms and nature-based learning experiences are being integrated into curriculums, fostering a love for nature in younger generations and promoting the practice of forest bathing.

In the business world, companies have begun to understand the importance of employee well-being and the role of nature in promoting productivity. Corporate retreats often include forest bathing experiences, allowing employees to disconnect from their screens and reconnect with the natural world.

As we navigate the complexities of the 21st century, the practice of forest bathing serves as a beacon, guiding us back to our roots and the simplicity and serenity of the natural world. It is a practice adapted and adopted by modern society, a testament to its timeless appeal and enduring relevance. As we move forward, it is clear that forest bathing will continue to play a crucial role in our lives, offering a sanctuary of tranquility in an ever-evolving world.

Reflecting on the Journey of Forest Bathing

As we draw the curtain on this exploration of forest bathing, we find ourselves standing at the edge of a green expanse, the whispers of the trees echoing the wisdom of centuries. From its ancient roots to modern adaptations, the forest bathing journey is a testament to the enduring bond between humans and nature. This bond has been nurtured and cherished across cultures and continents.

The genesis of forest bathing is as old as humanity itself. It is a practice born out of an intuitive understanding of the healing power of nature, an understanding that our earliest ancestors shared. They sought solace in the embrace of the forest, finding a balm for their weary souls in its serenity. This ancient wisdom passed down through generations, has been the bedrock upon which the practice of forest bathing stands.

The influence of the Japanese practice of Shinrin-Yoku has been instrumental in shaping the modern understanding of forest bathing. It has brought to the fore the therapeutic benefits of immersing oneself in the forest, of letting the symphony of nature envelop the senses. While still in its nascent stages, the science behind forest bathing has lent credence to what our ancestors instinctively knew - that the forest is a sanctuary of healing and rejuvenation.

The global spread of forest bathing reflects our collective yearning for a return to nature, a yearning that has been amplified in the face of the relentless pace of modern life. Across continents, people seek refuge in the forest, finding in its dappled light and rustling leaves a respite from the world's clamor.

The 21st century has seen a resurgence of interest in forest bathing, with modern adaptations making it accessible to a broader audience. From guided forest therapy walks to forest bathing retreats, the practice has evolved to meet the needs of a society increasingly disconnected from nature.

As we reflect on the forest bathing journey, we are reminded of the timeless wisdom of the forest. It is a wisdom that speaks of balance, harmony, and the interconnectedness of all life. It is a wisdom that invites us to step into the forest, to bathe in its tranquility, and to emerge rejuvenated, with a renewed sense of our place in the natural world. The journey of forest bathing is, in essence, a journey towards rediscovering our innate connection with nature, a journey that is as enriching as it is enlightening.

Chapter Summary

- Forest bathing, or Shinrin-Yoku, is rooted in the primal relationship between humans and nature. It involves a mindful immersion in the forest atmosphere, allowing the forest to cleanse the mind and rejuvenate the spirit.
- The concept of forest bathing is not new. It has been practiced by ancient cultures across the globe, from the Celts of Europe to the indigenous tribes of the Americas, who

revered the forest as a sacred space and a source of wisdom and healing.

- The practice of Shinrin-Yoku was developed in Japan during the 1980s as a form of ecotherapy. It had a transformative impact on Japanese society, improving physical health and fostering a deeper connection with nature.

- The science behind forest bathing began to be explored in the 1980s. Studies found that immersion in the forest environment could reduce blood pressure, lower cortisol levels, and improve concentration and memory. The key to these benefits lies in the natural compounds trees release, known as phytoncides.

- The concept of forest bathing has spread globally, resonating with people worldwide. Different cultures have embraced it, each adding unique interpretations and adaptations, yet united by the shared understanding of the forest's healing power.

- In the 21st century, forest bathing has been adapted and embraced in various ways globally. It has been integrated into urban environments, healthcare, education, and business, reassuring us of our inherent connection to the natural world.

- The global spread of forest bathing is a testament to our shared love for nature and our inherent need to be in harmony with the world. Despite our diverse cultures and landscapes, we are all drawn to the tranquility of the forest.

- The journey of forest bathing, from its ancient roots to its modern adaptations, is a testament to the enduring bond between humans and nature. It serves as a beacon, guiding us back to our roots and the simplicity and serenity of the natural world.

2

THE SCIENCE BEHIND FOREST BATHING

In the stillness of the forest, where the air is filled with the gentle rustling of leaves and the distant melody of birdsong, a profound connection is forged between us and the natural world. This connection, as ancient as our species itself, is the essence of forest bathing, a practice that invites us to immerse ourselves in the serene beauty of the woods. But what is it about this simple act that has such a profound impact on our well-being? What is the science behind the tranquility and rejuvenation we experience when we surrender ourselves to the forest's embrace?

Forest bathing, or Shinrin-yoku, is not merely a walk in the woods. It is a mindful immersion, a slow, deliberate journey into the heart of the forest. It is about letting the forest in, allowing it to fill our senses, touch our souls, and heal our bodies. It is about being present, aware, and one with the natural world.

The mysteries of forest bathing lie not just in the ethereal beauty of the forest but also in the intricate dance of biology, psychology, and chemistry that unfolds within us as we step into the woodland realm. This chapter will delve into the science behind forest bathing, exploring how our bodies react to the forest, the psychological impact of this practice, the healing power of phytoncides - nature's own medicine, and the role of our senses in engaging with the forest.

We will also take a global perspective, examining scientific studies worldwide that shed light on the myriad benefits of forest bathing. As we journey through this chapter, we will unravel the mysteries of forest bathing, revealing the science that underpins this soulful practice.

In the end, we hope to deepen your understanding and appreciation of forest bathing, encouraging you to embrace both the science and the soul of this rejuvenating practice. For in the heart of the forest, we find not just tranquility and wellness but also a profound connection to the very essence of life itself.

The Biological Response: How Our Bodies React to the Forest

As we step into the forest, leaving behind the concrete jungle and the rush of urban life, our bodies begin to respond to the serene embrace of nature in ways more profound than we often realize. This section delves into the fascinating biological response that occurs when we immerse ourselves in the forest, a phenomenon that forms the very foundation of forest bathing.

The moment our feet touch the soft, moss-covered forest floor, our heart rate begins to slow down, matching the tranquil rhythm of the forest. The air, rich with the scent of earth and foliage, fills our lungs, purifying them with each breath. This is not merely a poetic sentiment but a scientifically observed fact. Studies have shown that forest environments can significantly reduce blood pressure and heart rate, promoting relaxation and calm.

As we venture deeper into the forest, our bodies continue to respond to the forest's subtle cues. The gentle rustling of leaves, the distant call of a bird, the whisper of a breeze; these sounds, often drowned out in our daily lives, come alive in the forest. They act as gentle stimuli, engaging our auditory senses in a soothing symphony of natural sounds. This auditory engagement has been linked to a decrease in stress hormones, further enhancing the calming effect of the forest.

The forest air, imbued with natural compounds known as phytoncides, plays a crucial role in our biological response. These compounds, released by trees and plants, have been found to boost our immune system. As we breathe in the forest air, we inhale these phytoncides, which increase the activity of natural killer cells in our bodies, enhancing our overall immunity.

The forest's visual spectacle, a tapestry of greens, browns, and myriad hues, captivates our sight, providing a feast for our eyes. This visual engagement is not merely aesthetic; it profoundly impacts our mental well-being. The color green, predominant in forest environments, has been associated with feelings of relaxation and calmness, contributing to the overall therapeutic effect of forest bathing.

In essence, our bodies react to the forest in a symphony of responses, each note contributing to a state of relaxation, rejuvenation, and healing. This biological response, deeply ingrained in our evolutionary history, is a testament to our intrinsic connection with nature, a bond that forest bathing allows us to rediscover and strengthen.

The Psychological Impact: Forest Bathing and the Mind

A profound transformation begins in the heart of the forest, where the air is rich with the scent of pine and the rustle of leaves. As we step away from the clamor of the urban world and immerse ourselves in the tranquil embrace of nature, our minds begin to respond in ways that are as profound as they are healing. This section delves into the psychological impact of forest bathing, exploring how this simple yet powerful practice can soothe our minds, uplift our spirits, and rekindle our connection with the natural world.

The forest, with its verdant canopy and dappled sunlight, is a sanctuary for the mind. As we wander its paths, our thoughts begin to slow, mirroring the unhurried rhythm of the natural world. The constant barrage of stimuli that characterizes our modern lives fades away, replaced by the gentle symphony of the forest. This reduction in sensory overload allows our minds to relax, reducing stress and promoting a state of peaceful mindfulness.

Forest bathing also has a profound impact on our mood. The beauty of the natural world, with its intricate patterns and vibrant colors, can evoke feelings of awe and wonder that elevate our spirits and foster a sense of well-being. Moreover, being present in the forest, truly seeing, hearing, and feeling the world around us, can help ground us in the moment, alleviating anxiety and promoting a sense of calm.

The forest is not just a place of beauty but also a source of healing. Studies have shown that spending time in nature can boost levels of serotonin, the 'feel good' neurotransmitter, and reduce levels of cortisol, the 'stress hormone.' This can improve mood, sleep quality, and overall mental health.

Moreover, the forest can serve as a catalyst for introspection and personal growth. As we walk among the trees, we are reminded of the cycles of growth and decay, of the interconnectedness of all life. These reflections can foster a sense of perspective, helping us navigate challenges with greater resilience and grace.

In conclusion, the psychological impact of forest bathing is as diverse as it is profound. This practice offers many benefits for our minds, from reducing stress and improving mood to fostering mindfulness and promoting personal growth. As we continue to explore the science behind forest bathing, we come to understand that the forest is not just a place of beauty but a sanctuary for the soul, a place where we can reconnect with ourselves and the world around us in the most profound of ways.

The Healing Power of Phytoncides: Nature's Own Medicine

In the heart of the forest, a silent symphony of healing unfolds. It is a performance conducted by trees, a concert of invisible compounds known as phytoncides. These are volatile organic compounds, a natural elixir exuded by trees and plants, and a kind of botanical balm that permeates the forest air.

Phytoncides are not merely the scent of the forest; they are the forest's own medicine, a testament to the healing power of nature. They are the trees' defense mechanism against harmful insects and bacteria, but they serve a different purpose for us humans. They are a balm for our bodies, a salve for our souls, a tonic that can help to restore our health and well-being.

When we breathe in the forest air, we are inhaling these phytoncides. They enter our bodies, and their healing power begins to work its magic. Scientific studies have shown that exposure to phytoncides can boost our immune system, increasing the activity of our natural killer cells, the body's first line of defense against viruses and cancer.

Phytoncides also have a calming effect on our bodies. They can lower our blood pressure, reduce our heart rate, and decrease our levels of the stress hormone cortisol. They can help improve our mood, reduce anxiety, and promote peace and well-being.

The forest is not just a place of beauty and tranquility. It is a living, breathing pharmacy, a natural health spa that offers us a unique form of therapy. It is a place where we can immerse ourselves in the healing power of nature, where we can breathe in the forest's medicine and let it soothe our bodies and minds.

So, take a deep breath the next time you step into a forest. Breathe in the scent of the trees, the earth's fragrance, and the forest air's aroma. Know that you are breathing in phytoncides, nature's own medicine, and let their healing power wash over you. Let the forest bathe you in its healing light, cleanse your body and mind, and restore your health and spirit.

This is the science and the soul of forest bathing, a deep dive into the healing power of nature, a journey into the heart of the forest, a voyage of discovery and healing. It is a journey that can transform your life and bring you peace, health, and well-being. It is a journey that begins with a single step, a single breath, and a single moment in the heart of the forest.

The Role of the Senses: Engaging with the Forest

In the heart of the forest, where the air is pure, and the silence is only broken by the rustling of leaves or the distant call of a bird, our senses awaken in a profound and subtle way. In its tranquil majesty, the forest invites us to engage with it, not merely as passive observers but as active participants in a sensory symphony as old as life itself.

Often dulled by the monotony of urban life, our senses find a new vitality in the forest. The eyes, accustomed to the harsh glare of artificial lights, are soothed by the gentle play of sunlight filtering through the canopy of leaves. The myriad shades of green, the intricate patterns of bark, and the delicate beauty of a single leaf - all offer a visual feast that is both calming and refreshing.

The sense of smell, too, is awakened in the forest. The earthy scent of the soil, the fresh fragrance of pine needles, and the subtle perfume of wildflowers mingle in the air to create a natural, healing, and rejuvenating aromatherapy. This is not merely a poetic notion but a scientific fact. The forest air is rich in phytoncides, which have been proven to boost our immune system and enhance our well-being.

The forest also offers a symphony of sounds that is deeply soothing. The whispering of the wind through the leaves, the gentle rustling of small creatures in the undergrowth, and the melodic songs of birds create a natural white noise known to reduce stress and promote relaxation.

The sense of touch, too, is engaged in the forest. The rough texture of bark, the softness of moss, the coolness of a stream - these tactile experiences connect us directly with the natural world, grounding us in the present moment and fostering a sense of peace and well-being.

Finally, the forest engages our sense of taste. The tangy taste of wild berries, the sweetness of sap, the freshness of spring water - these natural flavors remind us of our deep connection with the earth and its bounty.

Engaging with the forest through our senses is not merely a pleasant experience but a powerful healing practice. It is a way of immersing ourselves in the natural world, reconnecting with our roots, and finding peace and rejuvenation in the heart of nature. It is, in essence, the soul of forest bathing.

Scientific Studies from Around the World

As we delve deeper into the verdant heart of forest bathing, it is essential to broaden our perspective and explore the global scientific studies that have been conducted on this subject. In its vastness and diversity, the world has embraced the healing power of the forest, and science has been the compass guiding this journey.

Numerous studies have been conducted in the land of the rising sun, Japan, where the practice of Shinrin-yoku, or forest bathing, was born. Researchers from the Nippon Medical School in Tokyo discovered that forest bathing significantly increases the activity of natural killer cells, an immune system component that fights cancer. This effect was found to last for more than 30 days after the forest visit, painting a picture of enduring health benefits that linger long after one has left the forest's embrace.

Across the Pacific, in the United States, a study by the University of Illinois revealed that residents with more green space in their environment reported lower stress levels and higher life satisfaction. This study, among others, underscores the profound impact of nature on our mental well-being.

In Europe, a study conducted in the Netherlands found that people who spent more time in green spaces had lower rates of depression and anxiety. Similarly, researchers in the United Kingdom found that being in nature, even briefly, improves mood, reduces feelings of stress or anger, and enhances physical well-being.

Venturing further to South Korea, a country that has established healing forests, a study found that forest bathing trips significantly reduced the scores for anxiety, depression, anger, fatigue, and confusion while improving vigor scores among participants.

These studies, scattered across the globe, are like the many trees of a forest. Each one stands tall, contributing to a more significant understanding, a global perspective that forest bathing is not merely a leisurely walk in the woods but a potent tool for health and healing.

As we conclude this section, let us remember that the science of forest bathing is as diverse and interconnected as the world's forests themselves. From the sun-dappled cedar forests of Japan to the towering redwoods of America, the whispering pines of Europe to the healing forests of Korea, each holds a piece of the puzzle, a unique contribution to our understanding of this remarkable practice. Let us sit quietly with the knowledge we have gained, like a forest bather beneath the trees, absorbing the world's wisdom.

Embracing the Science and Soul of Forest Bathing

As we close this chapter, we find ourselves standing at the edge of a vast expanse, the forest of knowledge we have traversed together. We have delved into the science behind forest bathing, unraveling the intricate tapestry of biological responses, psychological impacts, and the healing power of phytoncides. We have engaged our senses and explored the global perspective, gathering insights from scientific studies worldwide. Now, it is time to step back, breathe in the cool, crisp air, and embrace the science and soul of forest bathing.

In all its lush complexity, the forest is not merely a backdrop to our lives but an active participant in our well-being. It is a living, breathing entity that interacts with us deeply and profoundly. The science we have explored illuminates this relationship, shedding light on the myriad ways the forest nurtures, heals, and brings us back to ourselves.

As we have discovered, our bodies are finely tuned to respond to the forest. The rustle of leaves, the scent of pine, the dappled sunlight filtering through the canopy - these are not just sensory experiences but triggers for a cascade of biological reactions. They lower our blood pressure, boost our immune system, and flood our bodies with calm and well-being.

Our minds, too, are deeply affected by the forest. The quiet solitude, the gentle rhythm of nature, the sense of being part of something larger than ourselves - these experiences soothe our frazzled nerves, quiet our racing thoughts, and help us regain our mental equilibrium.

And then there are the phytoncides, those invisible, aromatic compounds that trees release into the air. They are nature's own medicine, working their subtle magic on us, strengthening our bodies, and fortifying our spirits.

But the science, as illuminating as it is, only tells part of the story. The soul of forest bathing lies in the experience itself - in the quiet moments of connection, the sense of awe and wonder, and the deep, abiding peace that settles over us as we immerse ourselves in the forest.

So, as we step out of the forest of knowledge and back into the world, let us carry with us the science and the soul of forest bathing. Let us remember that the forest is not just a place but a state of being, a way of connecting with the world and ourselves. Let us embrace the forest and, in doing so, embrace our own well-being. For in the end, the science and soul of forest bathing are the same - a testament to the profound, healing power of nature.

Chapter Summary

- Forest bathing is a mindful immersion into the forest, allowing it to fill our senses and heal our bodies. It is about being present and aware, fostering a deep connection with the natural world.
- Our bodies react to the forest in a symphony of responses, including a reduction in heart rate and blood pressure, a decrease in stress hormones, and an enhancement of our immune system through inhaling phytoncides.
- Forest bathing has a profound psychological impact, reducing stress, improving mood, fostering mindfulness, and promoting personal growth. It serves as a sanctuary for the mind, allowing for introspection and a sense of calm.
- Phytoncides, volatile organic compounds released by trees, play a crucial role in our biological response to the forest. They boost our immune system, lower our blood pressure, reduce our heart rate, and decrease our levels of the stress hormone cortisol.
- Engaging with the forest through our senses is a powerful healing practice. The forest offers a sensory symphony that is both calming and invigorating, grounding us in the present moment and fostering a sense of peace and well-being.

- Scientific studies worldwide have shed light on the myriad benefits of forest bathing, including increased activity of natural killer cells, reduced stress levels, higher life satisfaction, lower rates of depression and anxiety, and improved mood and vigor.
- The science of forest bathing is as diverse and interconnected as the world's forests themselves. Each forest, from the cedar forests of Japan to the redwoods of America, contributes to our understanding of this remarkable practice.
- The science and soul of forest bathing are the same - a testament to nature's profound healing power. The forest is not just a place but a state of being, a way of connecting with the world and ourselves.

3

THE ART OF MINDFUL WALKING: YOUR FIRST STEPS

W e begin our journey in the forest's heart, where the air is a symphony of subtle fragrances, and the light filters through the leaves in a dance of shadows and sunbeams. This is not a journey of miles and landmarks but one of awareness, presence, and being in the moment. This is the journey of mindful walking.

Mindful walking is an art that invites us to slow down, step away from the rush and clamor of our daily lives, and immerse ourselves in the tranquil embrace of nature. It is a dance with the forest, a gentle waltz where we move in harmony with the natural world's rhythm.

As we embark on this journey, we leave behind our worries, distractions, and preoccupations. We approach the forest with an open heart, ready to receive its wisdom. We are not merely observers but active participants in the forest's life. We are part of the forest, and the forest is part of us.

The journey of mindful walking is a journey of discovery. With each step, we uncover the secrets of the forest. We learn to see the beauty in the smallest leaf, to hear the music in the softest breeze, and to feel the life pulsating in the ground beneath our feet. We learn to see the world with new eyes, hear with new ears, and feel with a new heart.

Embracing the journey of mindful walking is embracing a new way of being, a new way of experiencing the world. It is a journey that can transform and bring us peace, joy, and a deep connection with the natural world. It is a journey that begins with a single step, a step taken with awareness, intention, and love.

So, let us begin. Let us step into the forest, into the heart of nature. Let us embrace the journey of mindful walking, and let the forest guide, heal, and awaken us to the beauty and wonder of the world around us.

The Rhythm of Nature: Tuning into the Forest's Heartbeat

As you stand on the threshold of the forest, take a moment to close your eyes and tune into the rhythm of nature. It is a rhythm that is both ancient and ever-present, a rhythm that pulses with life and vibrates with the universe's energy. It is the forest's heartbeat and is waiting for you to join its dance.

The rhythm of nature cannot be heard with the ears, but rather, it must be felt with the heart. It is a subtle, gentle pulse that resonates within the deepest parts of your being, a rhythm that is as much a part of you as your heartbeat. It is a rhythm that speaks of the interconnectedness of all life, the delicate balance between all living things, and the profound beauty that can be found in every moment.

To tune into the forest's heartbeat, you must first quiet your mind and open your senses. Let go of your thoughts, your worries, and your expectations. Allow your breath to slow and your body to relax. Feel the earth beneath your feet, the air on your skin, the sun's warmth, and the shade's coolness. Listen to the rustling of the leaves, the chirping of the birds, the whispering of the wind, and the silence beneath it all.

As you immerse yourself in the forest, you will begin to feel a rhythm, a pulse, a heartbeat. It may be faint initially, but it will grow stronger and more apparent as you walk mindfully. This is the rhythm of the forest, the rhythm of life itself. It is a rhythm that invites you to move in harmony with it, dance with it, and become one with it.

Tuning into the forest's heartbeat is not just about listening but also about feeling, connecting, and becoming one with nature's rhythm. It is about allowing the forest to guide, teach, and heal you. It is about surrendering to the moment, beauty, and magic in the forest.

So, take a deep breath, take that first step, and let the rhythm of the forest guide you on your journey of mindful walking. Let it lead you into tranquility, immersion, and rejuvenation. Let it awaken a sense of wonder, awe, and gratitude within you. Let it remind you of the simple joy of being alive and part of this beautiful, interconnected web of life.

And as you walk, remember: you are not just walking in the forest; you are walking with the forest, dancing to the rhythm of its heartbeat, becoming one with the rhythm of nature.

The First Step: Initiating the Dance with Nature

The first step into the forest is a moment of profound significance. It is the initiation of a dance with nature that is as old as the earth itself. As you cross the threshold from the manufactured world into the realm of the wild, you are not merely a spectator but an active participant in the grand ballet of life.

Imagine standing at the forest's edge, your feet firmly planted on the ground, your heart beating in rhythm with the earth's pulse. The air is cool and fresh, carrying the scent of damp earth and the subtle perfume of wildflowers. The trees stand tall and majestic, their leaves rustling softly in the breeze, whispering secrets of the forest. The sunlight filters through the canopy, casting dappled shadows on the forest floor. It is a scene of tranquil beauty, a symphony of sights, sounds, and scents that invites you to step in and join the dance.

As you take your first step, feel the texture of the earth beneath your feet. It may be soft, mossy, or rough and pebbled, but it is alive, teeming with countless life forms. Each step you take is a connection, a dialogue with the earth. It is a reminder that you are a part of this intricate web of life, not separate from it.

As you walk, let your senses guide you. Observe the play of light and shadow, the myriad shades of green, and the intricate patterns of leaves and bark. Listen to the rustle of leaves, the chirping of birds, the whisper of the wind. Feel the coolness of the air, the warmth of the sun, the gentle caress of the breeze. Smell the earthy scent of the forest, the fragrance of flowers, the aroma of pine and cedar. Each sensation is a thread in the tapestry of the forest, weaving a story of life, growth, and interconnectedness.

Walking in the forest is not about reaching a destination. It is about being present, being aware, being connected. It is about moving in harmony with nature, matching your rhythm to the rhythm of the forest. It is about opening your heart to the beauty and wonder of the natural world and allowing it to nourish and rejuvenate your spirit.

So take that first step. Initiate the dance with nature. Let the forest guide you, teach you, heal you. And as you walk, remember that you are not alone. You are part of the forest, and the forest is part of you.

The Path of Awareness: Observing, Feeling, and Connecting

As you step into the lush embrace of the forest, you are not merely a visitor but a participant in a grand, timeless ballet. The Path of Awareness is not a physical trail marked by signs or worn by the passage of countless feet. It is an internal journey, a shift in perception that allows you to truly see, feel, and connect with the forest around you.

Begin by allowing your senses to awaken. The forest is a symphony of sensations, a tapestry woven from countless threads of sight, sound, scent, and touch. Look around you. Notice how the sunlight filters through the leaves, casting dappled shadows on the forest floor. Observe the myriad shades of green, the intricate patterns of bark, and the delicate dance of a leaf falling to the ground.

Listen. The forest speaks in whispers and sighs, in the rustle of leaves and the distant call of a bird. Each sound is a note in the forest's song, a melody that has been playing since the dawn of time. Close your eyes and let the music wash over you, seeping into your soul and resonating with your inner rhythm.

Inhale deeply. The scent of the forest is a heady mix of earth and greenery, of life in its most primal form. It is the aroma of growth, of decay, of the endless cycle of life and death that sustains the forest. Each breath you take is a communion, a sharing of life force between you and the forest.

Reach out and touch the world around you. Feel the rough texture of bark beneath your fingers, the cool dampness of moss, the fragile delicacy of a leaf. Each sensation is a word, a phrase in the language of the forest. As you walk, let your hands brush against the plants and trees around you, a silent greeting between old friends.

The Path of Awareness is a journey of connection, a dance of unity between you and the forest. As you walk, you are not merely observing the forest but becoming a part of it. You are the forest, and the forest is you. This realization, this deep, profound connection, is the essence of forest bathing. It is a balm for the soul, a salve for the spirit, a reminder of our place in the grand tapestry of life.

As you continue your journey, remember this feeling. Carry it with you, not just in the forest but all aspects of your life. The Path of Awareness does not end when you leave the forest. It is a journey that continues, step by step, with each breath you take.

The Symphony of Silence: Listening to the Unspoken

A symphony of silence exists in the forest's heart, where the air is pure, and the light filters through the canopy in mottled patterns. It is not the absence of sound but rather a harmonious blend of subtle whispers that the forest breathes into existence. This symphony is the unspoken language of the forest, which speaks not to our ears but to our souls.

As you walk mindfully, let your senses become attuned to this symphony. Let the rustle of leaves underfoot become the percussion, the sighing of the wind through the branches of the woodwinds, the distant call of a bird, the soloist. Each sound is a note in the forest's composition, a piece of the tranquil melody constantly written and rewritten with each passing moment.

Listening to this symphony requires a quiet mind and an open heart. It requires you to step outside your thoughts, worries, and plans and be present in the moment. It requires you to listen with your ears and your entire being.

Feel the vibrations of the forest's song as they resonate within you. Notice how they ebb and flow with the rhythm of your breath and rise and fall with the beating of your heart. The forest speaks to you, sharing its wisdom, stories, and secrets.

In the silence, you may find answers to questions you didn't know you had. You may find peace amid turmoil and clarity amid confusion. You may find a sense of connection, a sense of belonging, a sense of home.

The symphony of silence is a gift from the forest, a reminder of the profound beauty and wisdom that exists in every moment if only we take the time to listen. As you continue your journey of mindful walking, carry this symphony with you. Let it guide your steps, nourish your soul, and remind you of the deep, unspoken connection between you and the natural world.

As we conclude this section, take a moment to reflect on your experience. What did you hear in the symphony of silence? What did the forest say to you? And most importantly, how will you carry this experience with you as you continue your forest bathing journey?

The Breath of Life: Synchronizing Your Breath with the Forest's Rhythm

In the heart of the forest, where the air is pure and the silence is profound, a rhythm pulses with life. It is a rhythm that is not heard but felt. It is the rhythm of the forest, the rhythm of life itself. Walking mindfully, you can synchronize your breath with this rhythm, creating a harmonious dance of life between you and the forest.

Breathing is the most fundamental of life's processes. It is the first thing we do when we are born and the last thing we do before we die. It is the constant companion of our existence, the silent witness to our joys and sorrows. And yet, we often take it for granted, forgetting its importance and potential for healing and rejuvenation.

In the forest, the act of breathing takes on a new dimension. The air is rich with the scent of pine and moss, the subtle perfume of wildflowers, and the earthy aroma of the soil. Each breath you take is a gift from the forest, a nourishing cocktail of oxygen and phytoncides, the natural chemicals released by trees that boost our immune system and reduce stress.

As you walk, focus on your breath. Feel the cool air entering your nostrils, filling your lungs, spreading life and energy throughout your body. Notice the slight pause, the moment of stillness, before you exhale, releasing the air back into the forest, a silent thank you for the gift you have received.

Try to match your breath with the rhythm of the forest. If you listen closely, you can hear it in the rustling of the leaves, the whispering of the wind, the distant call of a bird. It is a slow, steady rhythm, a peaceful lullaby that invites you to slow down, to let go of your worries and fears, to simply be.

Inhale deeply, drawing in the life-giving energy of the forest. Hold your breath for a moment, savoring the sensation of fullness, of being alive. Exhale slowly, releasing any tension or negativity, letting it flow out of you and dissolve into the forest.

With each breath, you become more attuned to the forest's rhythm, more connected to its life force. You are not just walking in the forest but becoming a part of it, a participant in the grand dance of life that unfolds in its depths.

As you continue your mindful walk, let your breath be your guide, your anchor in the present moment. Let it remind you of the simple joy of being alive and the beauty and wonder surrounding you. Let it fill you with gratitude for the forest and its many gifts, for the opportunity to walk in its embrace, breathe its air, and share in its rhythm.

In the forest, every breath is a celebration of life, a testament to the interconnectedness of all things. By synchronizing your breath with the forest's rhythm, you are not just forest bathing but engaging in a profound act of communion with nature, a sacred ritual of connection and renewal. In this dance of breath and rhythm, you will find peace, joy, and a sense of belonging that transcends words.

Reflecting on Your Journey and Looking Ahead to Future Forest Bathing Experiences

As we draw the curtain on this chapter, let us pause and reflect, like a tranquil pool mirroring the forest's verdant canopy. You have embarked on a journey of mindful walking, a dance with nature, where each step has been a gentle imprint on the forest floor, a silent conversation with the earth.

You have tuned into the forest's heartbeat, a rhythm that pulses beneath the bark of ancient trees and whispers through the rustling leaves. You have initiated a dance with nature that is as old as the wind and timeless as the sky. You have walked the path of awareness, observing, feeling, and connecting with the forest in a profound and deeply personal way.

You have listened to the symphony of silence, the unspoken language of the forest that speaks volumes in its quietude. You have synchronized your breath with the forest's rhythm, inhaling the crisp, clean air and exhaling any lingering stress or worry.

Now, as you stand at the edge of the forest, bathed in the soft, dappled light, take a moment to reflect on your journey. How do you feel? Has the forest changed you in any way? You may feel a sense of calm and tranquility, a renewed connection with nature, or a deeper understanding of yourself.

Looking ahead, imagine the countless forest bathing experiences that await you. Each visit to the forest will be a new adventure, a chance to deepen your connection with nature and continue your journey of mindful walking. The forest is a living, breathing entity, ever-changing with the seasons, and each visit will reveal new sights, sounds, and sensations to discover.

As you step out of the forest and back into the hustle and bustle of daily life, carry the forest with you. Let its tranquility seep into your everyday moments, its rhythm guide your steps, and its silence bring you peace. Remember, the forest is not just a place but a state of mind, a sanctuary where you can retreat whenever you need to recharge, rejuvenate, and reconnect with your true self.

So, until your next forest bathing experience, keep the forest in your heart, and let its wisdom guide you on your journey through life.

Chapter Summary

- Mindful walking is a journey of awareness and presence, where one immerses oneself in the tranquil embrace of nature, moving in harmony with the rhythm of the natural world.
- Tuning into the forest's heartbeat requires quieting the mind and opening the senses, feeling the rhythm of nature that speaks of the interconnectedness of all life.
- The first step into the forest initiates a dance with nature, where each step is a connection and dialogue with the earth, reminding us that we are part of this intricate web of life.
- The Path of Awareness is an internal journey that allows us to truly see, feel, and connect with the forest around us, becoming a part of it and realizing the deep, profound connection between us and nature.
- The Symphony of Silence in the forest is a harmonious blend of subtle whispers that speak not to our ears but to our souls, providing answers, peace, and a sense of connection.
- Synchronizing our breath with the forest's rhythm creates a harmonious dance of life between us and the forest, reminding us of the simple joy of being alive and the beauty surrounding us.
- Each visit to the forest is a new adventure, a chance to deepen our connection with nature and continue our journey of mindful walking, revealing new sights, sounds, and sensations to discover.
- The forest is not just a place but a state of mind, a sanctuary where we can retreat whenever we need to recharge, rejuvenate, and reconnect with our true selves.

4

THE SYMPHONY OF THE FOREST: ENGAGING YOUR SENSES

I n its tranquil grandeur, the forest extends an open invitation to all who seek solace, rejuvenation, and a deeper connection with the natural world. It is a realm where time seems to slow, where the frenetic pace of modern life is replaced by the gentle rhythm of the seasons, the ebb and flow of life in its most primal form.

As you step into this verdant cathedral, you are greeted by a symphony of sensations that engage each of your senses. The forest is not a silent, static entity but a living, breathing organism communicating in a language as old as the earth itself. It speaks in the rustle of leaves, the scent of damp earth, the soft touch of moss underfoot, the sight of dappled sunlight filtering through the canopy, and the taste of wild berries plucked straight from the bush.

This chapter is an invitation to immerse yourself in this symphony, to engage your senses in a way that perhaps you have not done since childhood. It is an invitation to experience the forest not as a mere backdrop to your outdoor activities but as a dynamic, sensory-rich environment that has the power to heal, inspire, and transform.

The forest is calling. Will you answer its call? Will you accept its invitation to step off the beaten path, wander beneath its towering trees, listen to its whispering leaves, breathe in its fragrant symphony, feel its textured canvas, and taste its hidden flavors?

If you do, you will discover that forest bathing is not merely a walk in the woods but a journey into the heart of nature itself. This journey engages all your senses and leaves you feeling refreshed, rejuvenated, and deeply connected to the world around you.

So, come. The forest is waiting. Its symphony is about to begin. And you, dear reader, are the honored guest.

The Visual Feast: Seeing the Forest in a New Light

In its grandeur and majesty, the forest is a visual banquet that invites us to partake in its splendor. As we enter its embrace, our eyes are greeted by a kaleidoscope of colors, shapes, and patterns dancing in the dappled sunlight. This is the forest's visual feast, a soothing and invigorating spectacle that invites us to see the world in a new light.

The forest is not merely a collection of trees but a living, breathing canvas of nature's artistry. Each tree, with its gnarled roots, sturdy trunk, and leafy canopy, is a masterpiece in its own right. The bark, with its intricate patterns of lines and cracks, is like an abstract painting, while the leaves, with their myriad shades of green, are like delicate brush strokes on a watercolor canvas.

As we delve deeper into the forest, our eyes are drawn to the play of light and shadow. The sun, filtering through the leafy canopy, casts a dappled pattern on the forest floor, creating a mesmerizing mosaic of light and dark. The shadows, shifting and changing with the sun's movement, add depth and dimension to the forest's landscape.

The forest is also a theater of movement. The rustling leaves, swaying branches, and scurrying creatures add a dynamic element to the forest's visual feast. Even the seemingly still trees are in constant motion, growing and changing with the seasons.

In the forest, we are invited to see not just with our eyes but with our hearts. Each element of the forest, from the towering trees to the tiny insects, is a testament to the beauty and complexity of nature. As we immerse ourselves in this visual feast, we are reminded of our connection to the natural world and our place within it.

The forest's visual feast is not just a spectacle to be observed but an experience to be savored. It invites us to slow down, look closely, and see the world with fresh eyes. It is a reminder that beauty is not just in the grand vistas but in the small details, the fleeting moments, and the subtle nuances. It is a call to see the world not just as it is but as it could be, filled with wonder, beauty, and possibility.

So, as you step into the forest, open your eyes wide. Let them feast on the forest's visual banquet. Let them be filled with the forest's colors, shapes, and patterns. Let them be captivated by the forest's play of light and shadow, its dance of movement and stillness. Let them see the forest and the world in a new light.

The Whispering Leaves: Listening to the Forest's Melody

In the heart of the forest, where the sunlight dapples through the lush canopy and the air is rich with the scent of earth and foliage, a symphony plays ceaselessly. It is a melody often overlooked, drowned out by the clamor of our thoughts and the noise of our busy lives. Yet, when we pause and allow ourselves to listen genuinely, we can hear the whispering leaves, the forest's own melody.

Close your eyes and lend your ears to the forest. At first, you might hear the apparent sounds: the rustling of leaves as a squirrel scampers up a tree, the distant call of a bird, and the soft sigh of the wind. But as you continue to listen and sink deeper into the tranquility of the forest, you will begin to discern the subtler notes of the forest's symphony.

The gentle pitter-patter of raindrops falling on the leaf-strewn floor, the soft rustle of a deer moving stealthily through the undergrowth, the faint hum of insects going about their day, the whispering leaves conversing with the wind. Each sound is a note, a chord, a phrase in the forest's melody.

Listening to the forest's symphony is about more than just hearing. It is about understanding, immersing yourself in the rhythm of nature, and allowing the forest's melody to resonate within you. It is about realizing that you are a part of this symphony, not a mere spectator.

The whispering leaves have much to say if only we take the time to listen. They speak of the changing seasons, the life that thrives in the forest, and the timeless wisdom of nature. They sing a song of peace, of harmony, of resilience.

As you listen to the whispering leaves and allow the forest's melody to wash over you, you will find a sense of calm enveloping you. Your thoughts will quieten, your heart will slow, your senses will awaken. You will feel rejuvenated, reconnected with the world around you, and reminded of nature's simple yet profound beauty.

So, the next time you find yourself in the heart of the forest, pause for a moment. Close your eyes, take a deep breath, and listen. Listen to the whispering leaves, to the forest's melody. Let it fill you, move you, and remind you of the beauty and tranquility in our world. For in the symphony of the forest, there is a song for each of us that speaks to our hearts and rejuvenates our souls.

The Fragrant Symphony: Smelling the Forest's Aromas

The forest is not just a visual spectacle but a fragrant symphony that plays a soothing melody to your senses. As you step deeper into the heart of the woods, allow your senses to be enveloped by the aromatic embrace of the forest.

Close your eyes and take a deep breath. The air is crisp, clean, and refreshing, a stark contrast to the artificial, recycled air of the urban jungle. The forest's perfume is a complex blend of scents, each note telling a different story, each aroma a character in the forest's narrative.

The earthy scent of the damp soil, rich and fertile, is the forest's foundation. It is the scent of life, growth, and the ceaseless cycle of birth, death, and rebirth. It is the smell of the forest floor, a complex tapestry woven from fallen leaves, decaying wood, and the countless organisms that call it home.

The sharp, resinous fragrance of pine needles pricks your senses, a poignant reminder of the evergreens that stand tall and unyielding, even in the harshest winters. It is a scent that speaks of resilience, endurance, and the forest's unwavering will to survive.

The sweet, floral aroma of blooming flowers wafts through the air, a delicate whisper of the forest's softer side. It is the scent of spring, renewal, and the forest's yearly rebirth in a riot of colors and fragrances.

And then there's the subtle, almost indiscernible scent of the forest's inhabitants. The musky smell of a deer that passed by, the tangy odor of a fox's den, the fresh scent of bird feathers. These scents remind you that the forest is not just a place but a living, breathing space teeming with life.

As you breathe in the forest's fragrant symphony, let it cleanse your lungs, mind, and soul. Let it ground you and connect you to the earth, nature, and the essence of life. And as you exhale, let go of your worries, stress, and fears. Let the forest's breeze carry them away, lost among the rustling leaves and towering trees.

The forest's fragrant symphony is a song of life, growth, and resilience. It is a song that speaks to the soul and resonates with the very core of our being. Once heard, it is a song that will forever echo in your heart, a lasting reminder of the forest's healing embrace.

The Textured Canvas: Feeling the Forest's Touch

The forest is a living, breathing entity, a textured canvas that invites you to explore its myriad sensations. It is a tactile symphony of textures ranging from the rough bark of ancient trees to the soft moss that carpets the forest floor.

As you step into the forest, your feet are greeted by the crunch of fallen leaves, the squish of damp earth, the solidity of rocks, and the springiness of moss. Each step is a new sensation, a new note in the forest's tactile symphony.

Reach out and touch the bark of a tree. Feel its roughness, its grooves and ridges, its knots and hollows. Each tree is written in the language of touch, a story of years weathered, storms survived, and seasons celebrated.

Run your fingers over the soft, velvety moss, a miniature forest within the forest. Each tiny frond is a world unto itself, a testament to the forest's ability to create and sustain life in the most unexpected places.

Feel the cool, smooth surface of a river stone, worn down by the relentless flow of water. It is a reminder of the forest's timeless rhythm, the ebb and flow of life that is its heartbeat.

Pick up a fallen leaf and trace its veins, a roadmap of life's journey from bud to maturity. It symbolizes the forest's cycle of life and death, a cycle that is as beautiful as it is relentless.

As you immerse yourself in the forest's tactile symphony, you begin to feel a deep connection with the natural world. You realize that you are not just a visitor in the forest but a part of it. You are a part of its symphony, a part of its story.

And as you leave the forest, you carry with you the memory of its touch, a lasting echo of the forest's symphony. It is a memory that will stay with you, a memory that will draw you back to the forest time and time again.

In the end, the forest's touch is not just a sensation but a connection, a bond that ties you to the natural world. It is a reminder of your place in the grand scheme of things and the beauty and wonder of the forest.

The Hidden Flavors: Tasting the Forest's Gifts

In the heart of the forest, where the sunlight dapples through the verdant canopy and the air is rich with the scent of earth and leaves, a hidden banquet of flavors is waiting to be discovered. This is not a feast for the eyes but for the palate, a subtle symphony of tastes that can only be experienced when one truly immerses oneself in the forest's embrace.

The forest is not merely a visual spectacle but a living, breathing entity that offers gifts to those willing to receive. The taste of the forest is as varied and complex as its ecosystem, a delicate balance of sweet, bitter, tangy, and earthy notes that dance on the tongue and awaken the senses.

Imagine the gentle kiss of morning dew on your lips, a taste as pure and refreshing as the forest air itself. The sweet nectar of a wildflower, sampled by a curious tongue, offers a burst of sunshine and summer in a single drop. The tart tang of a ripe berry, plucked from a bush heavy with fruit, reminds us of nature's generosity and the cycle of life and growth.

Even the air has a flavor, especially after a rain shower when the forest floor releases its earthy perfume. It's a taste as old as time, a primal memory that connects us to our ancestors who once roamed these woods and relied on these flavors for sustenance and survival.

The forest also offers more unexpected flavors. The slightly bitter taste of a leaf, the woody flavor of a twig chewed thoughtfully, the surprising sweetness of a sap droplet on the bark of a tree. These are not tastes we are accustomed to in our daily lives, but they are an integral part of the forest's rich tapestry of flavors.

As you wander through the forest, allow yourself to taste its gifts if it is safe to do so. Let your tongue become another exploration tool, another way to connect with the natural world. Each flavor is a note in the forest's symphony, a song that speaks of life, growth, and the eternal cycle of nature.

In tasting the forest's gifts, we not only engage our senses but also deepen our connection with the natural world. We become part of the forest, part of its symphony, and in doing so, we find a sense of peace and rejuvenation that can only be found in nature's embrace. The forest's flavors are a gift, a reminder of the simple, profound beauty of the natural world and the joy of being alive.

The Lasting Echo of the Forest's Symphony

As we draw the curtain on this immersive journey through the forest, we find ourselves standing at the edge of a profound realization. In its infinite wisdom and timeless beauty, the forest has offered us a symphony of experiences that have engaged our senses in ways we could have never imagined. However, the echoes of this symphony do not fade away as we step out of the forest's embrace. Instead, they linger, resonating within us and leaving a lasting imprint on our hearts and minds.

The forest's symphony is not merely a collection of isolated notes. It is a harmonious blend of sights, sounds, smells, textures, and tastes that have the power to transport us to a realm of tranquility and rejuvenation.

The visual feast of verdant greens and dappled sunlight, the whispering leaves sharing ancient secrets, the fragrant symphony of earth and bloom, the textured canvas of bark and leaf, and the hidden flavors of nature's bounty - each of these elements has played a unique melody in our forest symphony.

As we leave the forest, we carry these melodies with us. They become a part of us, subtly influencing our thoughts, emotions, and actions. They remind us of the forest's invitation to slow down, breathe, and be present. They inspire us to seek beauty in the ordinary, listen to the whispers of nature, and savor life's simple pleasures.

The echoes of the forest's symphony gently remind us of our connection to the natural world. They remind us that we are not separate from nature but integral to it. They encourage us to respect and protect the natural world, cherish its beauty and diversity, and honor its wisdom and resilience.

In the hustle and bustle of our daily lives, these echoes can serve as a soothing balm, a source of comfort and inspiration. They can help us navigate life's challenges with grace and resilience, reminding us of nature's healing power, mindfulness's importance, and the joy of simple pleasures.

As we conclude this journey, let us take a moment to express our gratitude to the forest for its generous gifts. Let us commit to carrying the echoes of the forest's symphony in our hearts, allowing them to guide, inspire, and heal us. Let us remember that the forest is not just a place but a state of mind, a way of being, and a source of endless inspiration and wisdom. And let us look forward to our next forest bathing experience, knowing that the forest will always welcome us with open arms, ready to share its symphony again.

Chapter Summary

- The forest is a living, breathing entity that offers a symphony of sensory experiences, inviting us to engage our senses in a way that can be profoundly healing and rejuvenating.

- The visual feast of the forest is a kaleidoscope of colors, shapes, and patterns that invites us to see the world in a new light, reminding us of the beauty and complexity of nature.
- The forest's symphony is not just audible but also a language of understanding, immersing oneself in the rhythm of nature, allowing the forest's melody to resonate within us, and realizing that we are a part of this symphony.
- The forest's fragrant symphony is a complex blend of scents that tells a different story, each aroma a character in the forest's narrative, reminding us of our connection to the natural world.
- The forest is a textured canvas that invites us to explore its myriad sensations, reminding us that we are not just visitors in the forest but a part of it, a part of its symphony, a part of its story.
- The forest offers a hidden banquet of flavors waiting to be discovered, each flavor a note in the forest's symphony, a song that speaks of life, growth, and the eternal cycle of nature.
- The echoes of the forest's symphony linger, resonating within us, leaving a lasting imprint on our hearts and minds and subtly influencing our thoughts, emotions, and actions.
- The forest's symphony serves as a gentle reminder of our connection to the natural world, encouraging us to respect and protect the natural world, cherish its beauty and diversity, and honor its wisdom and resilience.

5
_____

THE FOREST'S HEALING TOUCH: PHYSICAL AND MENTAL HEALTH BENEFITS

W e find a sanctuary in the serenity of the forest, where the air is rich with the scent of damp earth and the rustling leaves whisper ancient secrets. A sanctuary not built by human hands but by the patient, tireless work of nature herself. This is a place where we can shed the weight of our worries, where the clamor of the modern world fades into insignificance, replaced by the soothing symphony of the forest. This is the realm of forest bathing, a practice that invites us to immerse ourselves in the healing embrace of the woods.

Forest bathing, or Shinrin-yoku, is not about vigorous hiking or strenuous physical activity. It is about stillness, about allowing the forest to envelop us, to seep into our senses and touch our souls. It is about opening our hearts to the forest's healing touch, about letting the forest breathe life into us, rejuvenating our bodies and minds.

The forest is a living, breathing entity, a complex network of life that has evolved over millions of years. It is a world teeming with life, from the towering trees reaching for the sky to the tiny organisms that make their home in the rich, fertile soil. Each element of the forest, each leaf, each bird's song, and each ray of sunlight filtering through the canopy contributes to a healing environment that is as old as life itself.

As we step into the forest, we are stepping into a world that operates on a different rhythm, a rhythm that is in tune with the natural cycles of life. The forest's rhythm is slow, patient, and enduring. It is a rhythm that our bodies recognize that resonates with the deepest parts of our being. It is a rhythm that heals.

In this chapter, we will explore the healing power of the forest, delving into the physical and mental health benefits of forest bathing. We will learn about the forest's symphony and how the sounds of nature influence our well-being. We will discover the green prescription and understand the physical health benefits of forest bathing. We will find sanctuary for our minds, learning about the mental health advantages of immersion in nature. We will delve into the forest's aromatherapy, understanding the healing power of phytoncides. We will hear personal stories and experiences of the healing impact of forest bathing.

As we journey through this chapter, let us open our hearts and minds to the forest's healing touch, rekindling our ancient bond with the forest for holistic health. Let us embrace the forest's healing embrace, immersing ourselves in nature's tranquil, rejuvenating power.

The Forest's Symphony: How Nature Sounds Influence Our Well-being

In the heart of the forest, a symphony is perpetually in session. It is a concert that requires no tickets, no grand halls, and no formal attire. It is a performance that is as old as the earth itself, yet each rendition is unique, fresh, and invigorating. This is the forest's symphony, a harmonious blend of sounds that has the power to heal, rejuvenate, and inspire.

The forest's symphony is not merely an auditory experience; it is a sensory journey that begins with the gentle rustling of leaves, the distant call of a bird, the soft murmur of a brook, and the whispering wind. These sounds, subtle and soothing, have a profound influence on our well-being. They act as a balm to our overstimulated minds, offering a respite from the cacophony of our urban existence.

Scientific studies have shown that exposure to natural sounds can lower blood pressure, reduce stress hormones, and improve mood. The rhythmic patterns of nature, such as the repetitive sound of water dripping or leaves rustling, can induce relaxation akin to meditation. This is because these sounds often fall within the range of frequencies known to induce calm and relaxation in the human brain.

The forest's symphony also plays a crucial role in restoring our cognitive functions. The constant barrage of noise in urban environments can lead to cognitive fatigue, impairing our ability to focus and process information. On the other hand, the tranquil sounds of the forest can enhance our attention span and creativity. They provide a soothing backdrop that allows our minds to unwind, reset, and rejuvenate.

Listening to the forest's symphony is not a passive act. It is an immersive experience that invites us to engage with our surroundings and attune our senses to the subtle shifts in the forest's soundscape. It is an opportunity to practice mindfulness, to be present in the moment, and to connect with nature on a deeper level.

The forest's symphony is a testament to the healing power of nature. It is a gentle reminder of our intrinsic connection to the natural world, a connection that can nourish our physical and mental health. So, the next time you find yourself in the embrace of the forest, close your eyes, take a deep breath, and listen. Let the forest's symphony wash over you, heal you; let it play the melody of well-being in your heart.

The Green Prescription: Physical Health Benefits of Forest Bathing

In the heart of the forest, where the sunlight filters through the verdant canopy, casting dappled shadows on the forest floor, lies a potent remedy for our physical ailments. This remedy, as ancient as the forest itself, is the practice of forest bathing. The Japanese call it Shinrin-yoku, but regardless of the name, the essence remains the same - immersing oneself in the forest environment to reap its healing benefits.

The forest, in its tranquil grandeur, is a natural pharmacy. Its green prescription, written in the language of rustling leaves and whispering winds, offers many physical health benefits. Forest bathing is not merely a walk in the woods but a deliberate and mindful immersion in nature, a gentle communion with the forest that engages all our senses.

We inhale a cocktail of beneficial substances as we breathe in the forest air. Among these are phytoncides which, as we discovered in earlier chapters, are volatile organic compounds released by trees and plants. These substances, while serving as a plant's defense mechanism against insects and bacteria, profoundly impact our health. Research has shown that exposure to phytoncides boosts our immune system function by increasing the activity of natural killer cells, our body's defense against viruses and cancer.

The forest's green prescription also includes a dose of cardiovascular health. The calming effect of the forest environment reduces stress, a significant risk factor for heart disease. The serene forest setting lowers blood pressure, heart rate, and levels of the stress hormone cortisol. The result is a healthier heart, more attuned to the natural rhythms of life.

Moreover, forest bathing aids in combating obesity and diabetes. The physical activity involved, though gentle, helps in maintaining a healthy weight and improving insulin sensitivity. The forest's soothing ambiance encourages us to slow down and move at nature's unhurried pace, promoting a more active lifestyle.

The forest's healing touch extends to our respiratory system as well. The clean, fresh air of the forest, rich in oxygen and free from urban pollutants, relieves those suffering from respiratory ailments. Breathing in this air is like giving our lungs a refreshing cleanse, enhancing our overall respiratory health.

The green prescription of forest bathing is a testament to the healing power of nature. It is a call to return to our roots, to seek solace and rejuvenation in the embrace of the forest. As we immerse ourselves in this verdant sanctuary, we allow the forest to heal us, restore our physical health, and rekindle our ancient bond with nature.

The Mind's Sanctuary: Mental Health Advantages of Immersion in Nature

The forest is not a sanctuary built of stone and mortar, but it is alive, breathing, and ever-changing. It is a sanctuary for the mind, a haven where the tumultuous waves of thoughts and emotions find their calm.

The forest, with its serene beauty and tranquil silence, profoundly impacts our mental health. It is not just a place for physical exercise but a space for mental rejuvenation. The forest's gentle whispers, the rustling of leaves, and the soft murmur of a distant stream all work in harmony to soothe our minds, ease our worries, and transport us to peaceful contemplation.

When we immerse ourselves in this natural sanctuary, we are not merely observers but participants in a grand, interconnected dance of life. We become part of the forest, and the forest becomes part of us. This deep connection, this sense of belonging, can have a profound impact on our mental well-being. It can alleviate feelings of loneliness and isolation and foster a sense of inner peace and contentment.

Moreover, the forest, with its ever-changing seasons, serves as a gentle reminder of the impermanence of life. The vibrant green leaves of spring give way to the fiery hues of autumn, only to be replaced by the stark beauty of winter. This birth, growth, decay, and rebirth cycle can help us understand our life's transitions and changes. It can help us accept and embrace the ebb and flow of life rather than resist it.

The forest also teaches us the art of mindfulness. As we walk along its winding paths, listen to the symphony of nature, and breathe in the fresh, earthy scent of the forest, we become more present, more aware of our surroundings, and more in tune with our inner selves. This heightened awareness can help us manage stress, reduce anxiety, and enhance our mental health.

In the forest, we find a sanctuary for our minds, where we can heal, grow, and rejuvenate. It is a place where we can reconnect with ourselves, nature, and the rhythm of life. So, let us step into the forest, let us immerse ourselves in its healing embrace, and let us discover the profound mental health benefits that it has to offer.

The Forest's Aromatherapy: Understanding the Healing Power of Phytoncides

The green pharmacy of the forest is not housed within walls, nor does it have a counter where prescriptions are filled. Instead, its medicine is diffused in the air, a subtle, aromatic blend of organic compounds known as phytoncides.

Phytoncides, derived from the Greek words 'phyton' meaning 'plant' and 'cide' meaning 'kill,' are volatile organic compounds emitted by plants and trees. They serve as a natural defense mechanism against harmful insects and microorganisms. But these forest-born essences offer more than just protection for the trees; they are a balm for the human spirit and body.

You are also inhaling these phytoncides as you breathe in the forest air, rich with the scent of pine needles, damp earth, and the subtle perfume of wildflowers. They enter your body, whispering to your cells in a language as old as life itself. This is the forest's aromatherapy, a gentle yet powerful healer.

Scientific studies have shown that exposure to phytoncides can have significant health benefits. They can boost the immune system, increasing the activity of natural killer cells that help to fight disease. They can lower blood pressure, reduce stress hormones, and improve concentration and mental clarity.

Imagine, if you will, a walk in the forest as a therapeutic journey. With each step, you are moving deeper into a realm of healing. You draw in the forest's essence with each breath, allowing it to mingle with your own. The trees stand as silent therapists, their phytoncides a gift of health and well-being.

The forest's aromatherapy is a testament to the interconnectedness of all life. It reminds us that we are not separate from nature but a part of it. As we breathe in the forest's healing compounds, we participate in a cycle of mutual benefit, a dance of give and take that has been ongoing for millions of years.

In the end, understanding the healing power of phytoncides is about more than just recognizing the physical benefits they offer. It is about acknowledging our deep, intrinsic connection with the natural world. It is about embracing the forest's healing touch and, in doing so, finding a path to our own well-being.

Personal Stories of Forest Bathing's Healing Impact

Many have found solace, strength, and healing through the forest's embrace. This chapter is dedicated to their stories, to the transformative power of the forest that has touched their lives in profound ways.

Case Study 1

Our first tale is of a woman named Clara. A high-powered executive, Clara was a stranger to the concept of rest. Her life was a whirlwind of meetings, deadlines, and stress. One day, her body rebelled against the relentless pace, and she found herself bedridden, diagnosed with chronic fatigue syndrome. It was during her recovery that she discovered forest bathing. She began with short, gentle walks in the nearby woodland. The forest, she said, was like a balm to her frayed nerves. The rustle of leaves, the chirping of birds, the cool, clean air - it was as if each element of the forest was whispering to her, urging her to slow down, breathe, and heal. Over time, Clara regained her strength, and more importantly, she learned the value of balance and rest.

Case Study 2

Next, we have the story of Tom, a war veteran grappling with post-traumatic stress disorder. The memories of war were a constant shadow, a specter that haunted his days and nights. It was in the forest that Tom found a semblance of peace. He described the forest as a sanctuary where he could escape the ghosts of his past. The towering trees stood as silent sentinels, their steadfast presence a comforting reminder of the enduring power of life. With its gentle rhythms and soothing sounds, the forest became a place of refuge and healing for Tom.

Case Study 3

Lastly, we meet Lily, a young woman battling depression. She felt disconnected from the world in the depths of her despair, lost in a sea of sadness. It was her therapist who suggested forest bathing. Hesitant at first, Lily soon found herself drawn to the forest's tranquil beauty. She spoke of how the forest seemed to absorb her sorrow, replacing it with a sense of calm and serenity. The simple act of observing the forest, of being present and in the moment, helped Lily reconnect with herself and the world around her.

~

These stories, and countless others, are a testament to the healing power of the forest. They remind us that we are a part of nature, not apart from it. They urge us to seek solace in the forest's embrace, listen to its symphony, and breathe in its healing aromas. For in the heart of the forest, we can find our own hearts, healed and whole.

Rekindling Our Ancient Bond with the Forest for Holistic Health

As the sun dips below the horizon, painting the sky with hues of orange and purple, we find ourselves at the end of our journey, standing at the edge of the forest, our hearts filled with a newfound understanding and appreciation for its healing touch. We have explored the forest's symphony, green prescription, sanctuary for the mind, and unique aromatherapy. We have heard the personal stories of those who have found solace and healing in its embrace. Now, it is time to reflect on what we have learned and how we can rekindle our ancient bond with the forest for holistic health.

Our ancestors lived in harmony with nature, their lives intertwined with the rhythms of the earth and the forest. They understood the healing power of the forest, the way it could soothe a troubled mind, heal a weary body, and rejuvenate a tired spirit. This ancient wisdom, this deep connection with the forest, is something that many of us have lost in our modern, fast-paced lives. But it is not something that is lost forever. It is a bond that can be rekindled, a relationship that can be renewed.

Rekindling our bond with the forest begins with a simple step: stepping into the forest. It is about immersing ourselves in its beauty, tranquility, and healing energy. It is about letting the forest's symphony wash over us, letting its green prescription heal us, letting its sanctuary calm our minds, and letting its aromatherapy cleanse our spirits. It is about letting the forest touch, heal, and transform us.

But it is not just about taking from the forest. It is also about giving back, respecting and preserving the forest, and ensuring that future generations can feel its healing touch. It is about understanding that our health and the health of the forest are intertwined and that we are also healing ourselves by healing the forest.

As we leave the forest, we carry its healing touch with us. We carry its symphony in our hearts, its green prescription in our bodies, its sanctuary in our minds, and its aromatherapy in our spirits. We carry the stories of those who have found healing in its embrace, and we carry the hope of rekindling our ancient bond with the forest for holistic health.

The forest is not just a place. It is a healer, a sanctuary, a symphony, an aromatherapist. It is a part of us, and we are a part of it. By embracing the forest's healing touch and rekindling our ancient bond, we can find a path to holistic health that leads us back to our true selves, roots, and forests.

Chapter Summary

- Forest bathing, or Shinrin-yoku, immerses oneself in the forest environment, allowing the forest to envelop us and rejuvenate our bodies and minds. It operates on a rhythm that resonates with our being and promotes healing.
- The forest's symphony, a harmonious blend of nature sounds, profoundly influences our well-being. These sounds can induce a state of relaxation, restore cognitive functions, and enhance our attention span and creativity.
- The forest offers a green prescription for physical health. The calming effect of the forest environment also promotes cardiovascular health and aids in combating obesity and diabetes.

- Phytoncides, volatile organic compounds emitted by plants and trees, are a natural defense mechanism against harmful insects and microorganisms. Exposure to phytoncides can have significant health benefits, including boosting the immune system, lowering blood pressure, reducing stress hormones, and improving concentration and mental clarity.
- The forest serves as a sanctuary for our minds, helping to alleviate loneliness and isolation and fostering a sense of inner peace and contentment. It also teaches us the art of mindfulness, helping us manage stress, reduce anxiety, and enhance our overall mental health.
- Rekindling our ancient bond with the forest for holistic health involves immersing ourselves in its beauty, tranquility, and healing energy. It also involves giving back to the forest, respecting and preserving it for future generations.
- The forest is not just a place but a healer, a sanctuary, a symphony, and an aromatherapist. By embracing the forest's healing touch and rekindling our ancient bond with it, we can find a path to holistic health.

6

THE LANGUAGE OF TREES: UNDERSTANDING FOREST ECOLOGY

A s the first light of dawn gently pierces the veil of night, the forest awakens. The symphony of the forest begins with a soft prelude, a rustling whisper of leaves stirred by the morning breeze. It is an ancient and ever-new, timeless melody that speaks of life's enduring rhythm. This is the opening act of our journey into the heart of the forest, which will immerse us in the profound wisdom and healing power of trees.

The forest is not merely a collection of trees standing in silent isolation. It is a vibrant, interconnected community, a living, breathing entity that pulsates with life. Each tree, from the towering oak to the humble birch, plays a unique role in this grand orchestra. They are the musicians who create the symphony of the forest, which resonates with the deepest chords of our being.

As we delve deeper into the forest, we begin to perceive the subtle harmonies that underpin this symphony. The rustle of leaves is not just a random sound but a language, a form of communication that trees use to share vital information. The roots beneath our feet are not just anchors but intricate networks that connect trees in a web of mutual support and exchange. The air we breathe is not just a life-giving necessity but a testament to trees' crucial role in regulating our planet's climate.

The forest is a place of healing and rejuvenation. The simple act of walking among trees, of bathing in their presence, can have profound effects on our physical and mental well-being. This is the power of forest bathing, a power that is rooted in the very essence of trees.

As we journey through this chapter, we will explore the fascinating world of forest ecology. We will learn about the language of trees, the green network that binds them together, and their vital role in our world. We will discover the therapeutic power of trees and the importance of biodiversity in maintaining the health and vitality of our forests.

In the end, we will understand that the wisdom of the woods is not a distant, elusive concept but a tangible reality that we can embrace and incorporate into our lives. The symphony of the forest is not just a melody that we listen to but a song that we are a part of, a song that invites us to join in its harmonious dance.

So, let us begin our journey. Let us step into the forest, breathe in its healing air, listen to its symphony, and immerse ourselves in its tranquil, rejuvenating embrace. For in the heart of the forest, we will find not just trees but a reflection of our inner nature, a mirror that reveals our deep connection to the earth and all life.

The Rooted Conversations: How Trees Communicate

In the calm tranquility of the forest, a conversation is taking place. It is not one that we can hear with our ears, but rather, it is a dialogue that unfolds beneath our feet in the intricate network of roots and fungal threads that weave through the soil. This is the language of trees, a silent symphony of signals and messages that form the backbone of the forest's communication system.

Contrary to what we might initially believe, trees are not solitary beings. They are deeply interconnected, their lives intertwined in complex relationships across species and generations. Beneath the leafy canopy, in the stillness of the forest floor, trees engage in a ceaseless exchange of information, nutrients, and water, a process scientists have aptly named the "Wood-Wide Web."

This communication system is facilitated by mycorrhizal fungi, microscopic organisms that form symbiotic relationships with tree roots. The fungi extend their thread-like hyphae into the soil, creating a vast underground network connecting individual trees to one another. Trees can send and receive signals through this network, alerting each other to threats, sharing resources, and even nurturing their young.

Imagine a tree that harmful insects have invaded. Through the Wood-Wide Web, it can send out distress signals, alerting its neighbors to the danger. In response, the surrounding trees can ramp up their production of defensive chemicals, effectively inoculating themselves against the impending threat.

Similarly, when a tree is dying, it can redistribute its nutrients through the network, ensuring its legacy lives on in the forest it leaves behind. This is not a one-way street, however. Trees also receive nutrients and water from their neighbors in times of need.

In this light, the forest emerges not as a collection of individual trees but as a single, living organism, a community bound together by the language of roots and fungi. It is a testament to the power of connection, mutual aid, and cooperation, principles that are as vital to the health of a forest as they are to our own well-being.

As we immerse ourselves in the soothing embrace of the forest, let us remember this silent conversation that unfolds beneath our feet. Let us listen, not with our ears, but with our hearts, to the trees' wisdom and the lessons they teach us about interdependence, resilience, and the healing power of community. In the language of trees, we find a mirror to our humanity, a reminder of our deep-rooted connection to the natural world.

The Green Network: Exploring the Wood-Wide Web

In the heart of the forest, beneath the flourishing canopy and the dappled sunlight, lies a hidden world that hums with life. It is a world unseen, a world unheard, but a world that is as vital to the forest as the air we breathe. This is the world of the Wood-Wide Web, a complex network of roots and fungi that connects trees in a symbiotic relationship of shared resources and communication.

Imagine, if you will, the forest floor as a bustling city with its own highways and byways and traffic of nutrients and information. Standing tall and serene, the trees are not solitary entities but part of a vast, interconnected community. Their roots, intertwined with delicate threads of fungi, form an underground web that spans the entire forest.

This network, known as the mycorrhizal network, is the lifeline of the forest. It allows trees to share water, nutrients, and even information with each other. A tree suffering from drought can send a distress signal through the network, prompting its neighbors to share their water. A tree under attack from pests can warn its fellows, triggering a forest-wide defense mechanism. It is a system of mutual aid and cooperation, a testament to the interconnectedness of all life.

The Wood-Wide Web is not just a means of survival but also a means of nurturing. Older, more established trees, known as 'mother trees,' use the network to support their offspring, funneling nutrients to the saplings and helping them grow. It is a form of parental care that is as tender as it is essential, a gentle whisper of life in the quiet of the forest.

Exploring the Wood-Wide Web is like delving into the heart of the forest and the essence of its being. It is a journey of discovery, of understanding, of connection. It is a reminder that we, too, are part of a larger whole and are rooted in the earth and entwined with all life.

As we immerse ourselves in the tranquility of the forest, breathe in its healing air, and bathe in its soothing green light, let us remember the Wood-Wide Web. Let us remember the language of the trees, the forest symphony, and the woods' wisdom. Let us remember, and let us learn. For in understanding the forest, we understand ourselves. And in understanding ourselves, we find peace.

The Forest's Breath: The Role of Trees in Climate Regulation

A silent exchange occurs in the heart of the forest, where the sunlight filters through the leafy canopy. This is the forest's breath, a ceaseless cycle of inhalation and exhalation that is as vital to our planet's health as our respiration is to us.

Trees, in their serene and steadfast way, are the lungs of the Earth.

They inhale carbon dioxide, a greenhouse gas contributing to global warming, and exhale oxygen, the life-giving element that sustains most organisms. This process, known as photosynthesis, is a quiet yet powerful act of transformation that underpins the health of our global ecosystem.

Imagine, if you will, the forest at dawn. As the first rays of sunlight pierce the canopy, they touch upon the leaves, setting in motion a process as old as life itself. In their emerald splendor, the leaves absorb the sunlight, using their energy to convert the inhaled carbon dioxide and water into glucose, a sugar fueling the tree's growth and development. Oxygen, a by-product of this process, is released back into the atmosphere, a gift of life from the forest to the world.

But the forest's breath does more than regulate the composition of our atmosphere. It also plays a crucial role in climate regulation. By absorbing carbon dioxide, trees help to mitigate the impact of human-induced climate change. They act as carbon sinks, storing the absorbed carbon in their trunks, branches, leaves, roots, and the soil they stand in.

Furthermore, forests influence local and regional climates by regulating water cycles. Through a process known as transpiration, trees release water vapor into the atmosphere, contributing to cloud formation and precipitation. This nourishes the forest itself and impacts weather patterns and water availability in surrounding areas.

As we immerse ourselves in the tranquil embrace of the forest, let us remember the silent work being done by these towering sentinels of the Earth. Each breath we take is a testament to their ceaseless labor, a reminder of our deep and enduring connection with the natural world.

In understanding the language of trees, we come to appreciate their vital role in our world and our responsibility to protect and preserve them. For in their quiet, steadfast way, they are the guardians of our climate, the breath of our planet, the silent heartbeat of the Earth.

The Healing Canopy: The Therapeutic Power of Trees

In the heart of the forest, beneath the canopy, a realm of tranquility and healing exists. This is a world where the air is rich with the scent of damp earth and the whispers of leaves, where the sunlight filters through the foliage, casting dappled patterns on the forest floor. Here, in this serene sanctuary, we find the therapeutic power of trees.

Trees, in their silent, steadfast way, have been the guardians of our planet for millions of years. They have witnessed the passage of time, the changing of seasons, and the ebb and flow of life. Their roots delve deep into the earth, drawing nourishment and strength, while their branches reach towards the sky, embracing the light. They stand as symbols of resilience and growth, offering lessons of patience and perseverance.

But beyond their symbolic significance, trees hold a more tangible, physiological power to heal. Forest bathing is based on this very principle. It suggests that spending time under the canopy of a living forest can lead to significant health benefits through the presence of phytoncides in the forest air.

Moreover, the forest environment, with its soothing sounds of rustling leaves, chirping birds, and trickling streams, can have a calming effect on our minds. It can reduce stress, anxiety, and depression, promoting peace and well-being. In its quiet, unassuming way, the forest invites us to slow down, breathe, and reconnect with our inner selves and the world around us.

The healing power of trees extends to their ability to absorb carbon dioxide and release oxygen, purifying the air we breathe. They also act as natural filters, removing harmful pollutants and providing cleaner, healthier air. By doing so, they contribute to our physical health and play a crucial role in the health of our planet.

In the grand tapestry of life, trees are not merely passive observers. They are active participants, nurturing life, fostering growth, and offering healing. They speak a language of resilience and renewal, of connection and care. As we walk beneath their healing canopy, we are reminded of our place in the natural world, of the delicate balance, and of the profound wisdom held in the forest's heart.

So, let us listen to the trees' whispers, learn their language, and embrace the healing power they offer. In doing so, we not only nurture our own health and well-being but also contribute to the health and sustainability of our planet.

The Forest's Guardians: The Importance of Biodiversity

The forest is home to towering trees and the myriad creatures that call the forest their home. They are the guardians of the forest, each playing a vital role in maintaining the delicate balance of this complex ecosystem. This section delves into the importance of biodiversity, the forest's guardians, in the grand symphony of the woods.

Biodiversity, in its simplest form, refers to the variety of life in a particular habitat or ecosystem. In a forest, it encompasses everything from the smallest microorganism in the soil to the largest mammal that roams its depths. Each species, no matter how seemingly insignificant, contributes to the overall health and resilience of the forest.

Consider the humble earthworm, often overlooked and underappreciated. These tiny creatures are the unsung heroes of the forest floor, tirelessly working to break down organic matter and enrich the soil. This process nourishes the trees and supports the growth of other plants, creating a lush understory that provides food and shelter for a host of animals.

Similarly, the larger forest inhabitants, such as deer and birds, play their part in the life cycle. They help in the dispersal of seeds, ensuring the propagation of trees and other plant species. Predators, in turn, keep the population of these herbivores in check, preventing overgrazing and maintaining the diversity of plant life.

The forest's guardians also include the trees themselves. Different tree species offer different resources, from food to shelter, attracting wildlife and supporting a rich tapestry of life. The biodiversity of trees also enhances the forest's resilience, enabling it to withstand diseases and pests that could decimate a monoculture.

In essence, biodiversity is the lifeblood of the forest. It is a testament to the interconnectedness of all living things, a delicate dance of give-and-take that has been perfected over millennia. It is a reminder that every creature, plant, and microorganism has a role in the grand scheme of things.

As we immerse ourselves in the tranquility of the forest, let us not forget the silent guardians surrounding us. Let us appreciate the biodiversity that breathes life into the forest, makes each visit a unique experience, and teaches us the value of balance and harmony. By understanding and respecting these guardians, we enrich our forest bathing experience and contribute to preserving these magnificent ecosystems for generations to come.

Embracing the Wisdom of the Woods

As we draw the curtain on this verdant journey, we find ourselves standing at the edge of the forest, our senses heightened, our minds enriched, and our hearts filled with a newfound respect for the wisdom of the woods. In its tranquil silence, the forest has spoken volumes, teaching us lessons that resonate deep within our souls.

The forest is not merely a collection of trees, plants, and wildlife. It is a living, breathing entity, a complex network of life that thrives on cooperation and mutual support. The trees' roots entwined in a silent conversation have shown us the power of connection and community. They whisper to each other through the wood-wide web, sharing resources, sending warnings, and nurturing their young. This interconnectedness, this unity in diversity, is a lesson we can carry into our lives, reminding us of the strength in unity and the beauty that blooms in diversity.

The forest's breath, the gentle rustle of leaves in the wind, and the soft sigh of oxygen released into the atmosphere have taught us about trees' vital role in climate regulation. They are the lungs of our planet, inhaling carbon dioxide and exhaling life-giving oxygen, a silent yet powerful testament to the importance of balance in nature and our lives.

The healing canopy of the forest, with its therapeutic power, has shown us the path to rejuvenation and well-being. Forest bathing, the simple act of immersing oneself in the forest atmosphere, can heal our bodies, calm our minds, and soothe our spirits. It is a gentle reminder of the healing power of nature and the importance of reconnecting with our roots.

The forest's guardians, the myriad species that call it home, have shown us the importance of biodiversity. Each creature, no matter how small, plays a crucial role in maintaining the balance of the ecosystem.

Their presence reminds us of our responsibility to protect and preserve the natural world, for in its survival lies our own.

As we step out of the forest, we carry its wisdom, lessons, and tranquility with us. We leave behind the noise and chaos of our everyday lives and enter a world of serenity and harmony. We have learned to listen to the trees' language, understand their silent conversations, appreciate their role in our world, and embrace their wisdom.

In its timeless wisdom, the forest has shown us the way to a more mindful, balanced, and fulfilling life. It has taught us to value connection, cherish diversity, respect the balance of nature, and embrace the healing power of the natural world. As we move forward, let us carry these lessons in our hearts, live in harmony with nature, and embrace the wisdom of the woods.

Chapter Summary

- The forest is a vibrant, interconnected community of trees, each playing a unique role in the ecosystem. The rustle of leaves is a form of communication, and the roots form intricate networks that connect trees in a web of mutual support and exchange.
- Trees communicate through a complex network of roots and fungal threads called the "Wood-Wide Web." This silent symphony of signals and messages allows trees to share vital information, nutrients, and water.
- The Wood-Wide Web is a lifeline of the forest, allowing trees to share resources and information. It also enables older, established trees to support their offspring, demonstrating a form of parental care.
- Trees play a crucial role in climate regulation. Through photosynthesis, they absorb carbon dioxide and release oxygen, acting as the lungs of the Earth. They also influence local and regional climates by regulating water cycles.

- Spending time in the forest, or forest bathing, can have significant health benefits. The forest air is filled with phytoncides, which boost immune system function, reduce blood pressure, and improve mood and sleep patterns.
- Biodiversity is vital to the health and resilience of the forest. Every creature, plant, and microorganism plays a role in the ecosystem, contributing to the overall balance and harmony of the forest.
- The forest teaches us valuable lessons about interdependence, resilience, and the healing power of community. It reminds us of our deep-rooted connection to the natural world and our responsibility to protect and preserve it.
- The forest offers a path to rejuvenation and well-being, teaching us to value connection, cherish diversity, respect the balance of nature, and embrace the healing power of the natural world. It shows us the way to a more mindful, balanced, and fulfilling life.

7

FOREST BATHING THROUGH THE SEASONS: A YEAR-ROUND GUIDE

I n the heart of the forest, time dances to a different rhythm. In its infinite wisdom, the forest does not adhere to the ticking of clocks or the turning of calendar pages. Instead, it follows a more ancient, more profound cadence - the symphony of the seasons. Each season's unique melody brings a new chapter in the forest's ongoing saga, a fresh perspective to our forest bathing journey.

Forest bathing is an immersive, sensory experience that invites us to connect with the forest's soul, to bathe in its essence. As we step into the forest, we step into a world that is alive, breathing, and ever-changing. We become part of the forest's narrative, woven into its tapestry of life.

The forest's seasonal symphony is a celebration of change, a testament to the forest's resilience and adaptability. Each season brings its own unique charm, its own distinct energy. Winter's hush, spring's awakening, summer's embrace, and autumn's farewell play a vital role in the forest's lifecycle, each offering a unique backdrop for our forest bathing experience.

With its silent serenity, winter invites us into a world of stillness, where every snow-cloaked tree stands as a sentinel of tranquility. With its rebirth of life, spring paints the forest in green hues as life stirs amidst the verdant canopies. With its warm whisper, summer bathes the forest in golden light as sun-dappled leaves sway in the gentle breeze. With its rustling lullaby, autumn bids farewell with a cascade of falling foliage, a spectacle of colors that warms the heart as the air grows crisp.

As we journey through the seasons, we learn to adapt, to flow with the forest's ebb and flow. We learn to embrace the changing seasons, find beauty in each moment, and see the forest not just as a static entity but as a dynamic, living organism that grows, changes, and evolves.

This chapter will explore the forest's seasonal symphony, guiding you through a year-round forest bathing experience. We will delve into the unique charm of each season, offering insights and tips on adapting your forest bathing practice to the changing seasons.

So, let us embark on this journey together, immersing ourselves in the forest's seasonal symphony, bathing in its tranquil, rejuvenating energy. Let us embrace the forest's endless cycle of renewal and reflection, finding peace, solace, and connection in its ever-changing beauty.

Winter's Hush: The Silent Serenity of Snow-Cloaked Trees

As the last leaves of autumn fall, the forest transitions into a season of profound tranquility. With its hushed whispers and serene landscapes, winter offers a unique experience for the forest bather. This season invites you to immerse yourself in the quiet beauty of the winter forest, a world transformed by a blanket of snow and the crisp, clean air.

The forest in winter is a realm of stillness, where a profound silence replaces the usual rustling and chirping. This silence is not empty but instead filled with peace and calm that can only be found in the heart of winter. Now devoid of their leafy attire, the trees stand as stoic sentinels, their bare branches reaching out to the sky in silent prayer. Each one is adorned with a delicate layer of snow, transforming the forest into a monochrome masterpiece.

As you step into this winter wonderland, the crunch of your footsteps on the fresh snow is the only sound that dares to break the silence. The crisp and refreshing air fills your lungs with a cool freshness that revitalizes your senses. Each breath you take reminds you of the forest's enduring life force, even amid winter's slumber.

Standing tall and serene, the snow-cloaked trees invite you to pause and reflect. Their stark beauty against the winter sky is a testament to the forest's resilience. They stand firm, weathering the winter's chill, their roots buried deep in the frozen earth, waiting patiently for the return of spring.

You find a space for introspection in the heart of the forest, surrounded by the silent serenity of snow-cloaked trees. The quietness allows your thoughts to flow freely, unencumbered by distractions. In its winter guise, the forest becomes a mirror, reflecting your inner self back to you.

Winter's hush is not a time of dormancy but rather a season of introspection and rejuvenation. It is a time to slow down, to breathe in the crisp air, to marvel at the beauty of the snow-cloaked trees, and to find peace in the forest's silent serenity. As you immerse yourself in this winter forest bathing experience, you become a part of the forest's quiet symphony, your heart beating in time with the silent rhythm of the winter woods.

Spring's Awakening: The Rebirth of Life

As winter's icy grip begins to loosen, the forest stirs from its slumber, heralding the arrival of spring. Spring is a tribute to this season of renewal, when the forest bathes itself in a fresh palette of vibrant hues, and the air is filled with the sweet perfume of blossoming flowers.

As you step into the forest during spring, you are greeted by a symphony of sounds. The once-silent woods are now alive with the melodious chirping of birds, the rustling of leaves, and the distant murmur of a babbling brook. The forest is celebrating the end of winter's reign and the arrival of a season of growth and rebirth.

Once bare and skeletal, the trees are now adorned with a lush canopy of leaves. The verdant foliage forms a natural cathedral, its arches reaching toward the sky, filtering the sunlight into a soft, mottled glow that dances on the forest floor. The sight is a feast for the eyes, a tableau of varying shades of green, from the pale, almost translucent hue of new leaves to the deep, rich color of mature foliage.

Beneath the towering trees, the forest floor is a carpet of wildflowers, their delicate petals unfurling to greet the sun. Each flower is a testament to the forest's resilience, a symbol of life's ability to endure even the harshest winters. As you walk amongst them, you can't help but feel a sense of awe and wonder at the sheer beauty of nature's handiwork.

Spring is also a time of activity for the forest's inhabitants. Squirrels scamper across the forest floor, their tiny paws leaving a trail in the soft, damp earth. Birds flit from branch to branch, their songs echoing through the trees. Deer graze peacefully in the clearings, their fawns taking their first tentative steps under the watchful eyes of their mothers.

Forest bathing in spring is a sensory experience, a chance to immerse yourself in the forest's sights, sounds, and smells. It is a time to slow down, to breathe in the fresh, crisp air, to listen to the rustling of leaves, to feel the warmth of the sun on your skin, and to marvel at the beauty of the forest in full bloom.

As you leave the forest, you carry with you a sense of peace and tranquility, a renewed appreciation for the simple beauty of nature, and a profound understanding of the cycle of life and renewal that the forest embodies. Spring's awakening is not just a season; it is a state of mind, a reminder of the endless cycle of life, death, and rebirth that is the essence of our existence.

Summer's Embrace: The Warm Whisper of Sun-Dappled Leaves

As the wheel of the year turns, the forest shifts from the vibrant rebirth of spring to the languid embrace of summer. The air is thick with sun-warmed pine and the sweet, heady perfume of blooming wildflowers. The forest is alive with a symphony of sounds, from the gentle rustle of leaves to the distant call of a bird. This is the season of summer's embrace, when the forest is lush and inviting, a time for the warm whisper of sun-dappled leaves.

The forest in summer is a place of abundance and vitality. The trees, now fully clothed in their verdant finery, stand tall and proud, their leaves a vibrant tapestry of greens. The sunlight filters through the canopy, casting a dotted pattern on the forest floor, a dance of light and shadow that changes with the passing hours. This is the forest's summer song, a melody composed of light, warmth, and the ceaseless rhythm of life.

Forest bathing in summer is a sensory feast. The touch of the warm breeze against your skin, the taste of sweet berries plucked straight from the bush, the sight of butterflies flitting among the flowers, the sound of leaves whispering secrets to each other as they sway in the wind, the scent of earth and leaves and life - all these combine to create an experience that is both grounding and uplifting.

Walking through the forest in summer, you can't help but feel a deep connection to the world around you. Each step takes you deeper into the heart of the forest; each breath draws the essence of summer into your being. Summer is a time for basking in the sun's warmth, lying on a bed of soft moss and watching the clouds drift by, and letting the forest's summer embrace wash over you and fill you with a sense of peace and contentment.

Summer's embrace is a time of growth and abundance, a time to celebrate the fullness of life. It is a time to immerse yourself in the forest's vibrant energy, to let the warm whisper of sun-dappled leaves guide you on your forest bathing journey. As you walk among the trees, let the forest's summer song fill your heart and soul and remind you of the beauty and wonder of the world around you. This is the magic of forest bathing in summer, which is there for all willing to open their hearts and minds to the forest's gentle embrace.

Autumn's Farewell: The Rustling Lullaby of Falling Foliage

As the year gently pivots towards its twilight, the forest begins to prepare for its grandest spectacle. Autumn, the season of mellow fruitfulness, arrives with a painter's palette, drenching the woodland in hues of gold, crimson, and amber. This time of the year invites you to immerse yourself in the forest's autumnal embrace when the trees bid farewell to their leafy crowns and the forest floor becomes a tapestry of fallen leaves.

The forest in autumn is a symphony of rustling leaves, a lullaby that sings of the year's maturity. Each leaf that falls is a note in this melody, a gentle reminder of the impermanence of life and the beauty of change. As you walk through the forest, the crunch of leaves underfoot and the whisper of the wind through the boughs create a soothing soundtrack, a natural music that invites introspection and tranquility.

The air in autumn carries a distinct crispness, a coolness that contrasts with the warmth of summer's lingering touch. It is a sensory delight, filled with the earthy scent of decaying leaves, the tang of ripening fruits, and the subtle hint of wood smoke from distant hearths. As you breathe in, you are not just inhaling air but the very essence of the forest, a blend of life, death, and rebirth that is as intoxicating as it is rejuvenating.

Forest bathing in autumn is a feast for the eyes. The trees, once a uniform green, now blaze with color, each one a testament to nature's artistry. The sunlight, softened by the shorter days, filters through the leaves, casting a golden glow that seems to set the forest alight. It is a breathtaking and humbling spectacle, a reminder of nature's ability to transform and renew.

As you immerse yourself in this autumnal wonderland, allow yourself to become a part of the forest's farewell. Feel the leaves crunch underfoot, listen to the rustling lullaby of the falling foliage, breathe in the crisp air, and let your eyes feast on the riot of colors. This is forest bathing at its most profound, a chance to connect with nature at a time of change and reflection when the forest prepares for the hush of winter in its quiet, beautiful way.

Autumn's farewell is not an end but a transition, a pause before the cycle begins anew. It is a time to reflect, to appreciate, and to prepare. As the leaves fall and the forest quiets, we are reminded of the beauty of change, the inevitability of cycles, and the rejuvenating power of nature. So, as you walk through the autumn forest, let its rustling lullaby soothe your soul, and let its vibrant colors ignite your spirit. For in the heart of the forest, every season is a new beginning, and every farewell is but a prelude to a new hello.

The Ebb and Flow of Forest Bathing: Adapting to Change

Just as the forest breathes with the rhythm of the seasons, so should our practice of forest bathing adapt and flow with the changing times. Each season brings a unique palette of sensations, a distinct symphony of sounds, and a kaleidoscope of colors that can enrich our experience of the forest in profound ways.

In the heart of winter, when the forest is hushed under a blanket of snow, our forest bathing practice might take on a more contemplative tone. The silence of the snow-cloaked trees invites us to slow down, to listen more deeply, and to find peace in the stillness. We might choose to walk more slowly, to sit quietly by a frozen stream, or to stand in awe of the stark beauty of the winter landscape.

As spring unfurls its green tendrils, our forest bathing practice can awaken alongside the forest. The rebirth of life amidst the verdant canopies invites us to open our senses to the vibrant energy of growth and renewal. We may engage more actively with the forest, to touch the tender new leaves, to smell the fresh blossoms, or to listen to the chorus of birdsong.

In the embrace of summer, when the forest is dappled with warm sunlight, our forest bathing practice can become a celebration of abundance. The whisper of sun-dappled leaves invites us to bask in the joy of the present moment, feel the sun's warmth on our skin, and taste the sweet fruits of the season.

As autumn bids farewell, our forest bathing practice can become a gentle lullaby of letting go. The rustling of falling foliage invites us to reflect on the impermanence of life, appreciate the beauty of decay, and prepare for winter's stillness.

In this ebb and flow of forest bathing, we learn to adapt to the changing seasons, to honor the cycles of nature, and to find our place within the endless cycle of renewal and reflection. Just as the forest changes with the seasons, so too do we. And in this dance with the forest, we find a deeper connection to the world and the rhythms of our lives.

The Endless Cycle of Renewal and Reflection

As we draw the curtain on our year-long journey through the forest, we find ourselves standing at the threshold of a profound understanding. We have bathed in the forest's seasonal symphony; each note a whispering leaf, a rustling branch, a silent snowfall. We have learned to listen to the forest's heartbeat, to feel its pulse in the rhythm of the seasons. We have discovered that forest bathing is not merely a practice but a way of life, a way of being in harmony with the natural world.

Winter's hush taught us the beauty of silence and the serenity of solitude. We learned to appreciate the stark elegance of snow-cloaked trees, their bare branches reaching out to the grey skies like skeletal hands. We learned to find warmth in the cold and comfort in the quiet.

Spring's awakening brought us the rebirth of life and the resurgence of hope. We watched as the forest shook off its winter slumber as the verdant canopies unfurled their leaves to the sky. We learned to appreciate the miracle of growth, the magic of renewal.

Summer's embrace wrapped us in the warm whisper of sun-dappled leaves, the gentle hum of life in full bloom. We learned to appreciate nature's abundance and the earth's generosity.

Autumn's farewell sang us the rustling lullaby of falling foliage, the poignant beauty of endings. We learned to appreciate the cycle of life and the inevitability of change.

Through the ebb and flow of forest bathing, we have learned to adapt to the changing seasons to find peace in the constant flux of life. We have learned to breathe with the forest, to live with the forest, to be one with the forest.

As we conclude our year in the forest, we find ourselves not at the end but at the beginning of a new cycle. The forest has taught us that there are no true endings, only moments of reflection and renewal. We have learned to see each ending as a new beginning, each farewell as a new awakening.

In the forest, we have found a sanctuary of tranquility and rejuvenation. We have found a home. And as we step out of the forest, we carry its lessons with us, its wisdom etched into our hearts. We carry the forest within us, its rhythm pulsing in our veins, its melody humming in our souls.

And so, we bid farewell to the forest, not with a sense of loss but a sense of gratitude, for the forest has given us more than we could ever give back. It has given us a sense of belonging, a sense of peace, a sense of self. It has given us a year of memories and a lifetime of lessons.

And as we step into the new year, we step with the forest. We step with the seasons. We step with the rhythm of life. We step into the endless cycle of renewal and reflection. We step with the forest, and the forest steps with us.

Chapter Summary

- The forest's seasonal symphony is a testament to its resilience and adaptability, with each season offering a unique backdrop for the practice of forest bathing.
- The practice of forest bathing should adapt and flow with the changing seasons, each offering a unique palette of sensations, sounds, and colors that can enrich the experience of the forest.
- Winter's hush invites introspection and peace, with the silent serenity of snow-cloaked trees offering a space for contemplation and rejuvenation.
- Spring's awakening is a sensory experience filled with the vibrant energy of growth and renewal, offering a chance to immerse oneself in the forest's sights, sounds, and smells in full bloom.
- Summer's embrace celebrates abundance and vitality, with the warm whisper of sun-dappled leaves providing a grounding and uplifting forest bathing experience.
- Autumn's farewell is a gentle lullaby of letting go, with the rustling of falling foliage inviting reflection on the impermanence of life and the beauty of change.
- Forest bathing is not merely a practice but a way of life, a way of being in harmony with the natural world and learning to

adapt to the changing seasons, honor the cycles of nature, and find our place within the endless cycle of renewal and reflection.

- The forest offers a sanctuary, a place of tranquility and rejuvenation, and through the practice of forest bathing, we can carry its lessons and wisdom with us, finding a sense of belonging, peace, and self.

8

FOREST BATHING WITH CHILDREN: CULTIVATING A LOVE FOR NATURE

A world of wonder awaits in the peaceful tranquility of the forest. This world, teeming with life and mystery, holds a special allure for children. Their eyes light up with curiosity and delight as they explore, their senses awakened by the forest's myriad sights, sounds, and scents. This is the joy of introducing children to forest bathing. This practice immerses them in nature's beauty and nurtures their physical, emotional, and cognitive development.

Forest bathing is not about hiking or exercising but about being present, slowing down, and allowing the forest to envelop you, speaking to you in its quiet, serene language. It is about letting the forest air, filled with the soothing scent of pine and earth, cleanse your spirit and rejuvenate your senses.

Introducing children to forest bathing is akin to opening the door to a magical realm where they can touch the rough bark of a tree, listen to the whispering wind, watch a squirrel scamper up a branch, and feel the cool forest floor beneath their feet. It is a realm where they can learn, grow, and form a deep, lasting bond with nature.

The joy of introducing children to forest bathing lies in the immediate happiness and excitement it brings them and the long-term benefits it offers. It is a joy that stems from knowing that you are giving them a gift that will enrich their lives and help them become more mindful, more respectful of nature, and more in tune with their own senses and emotions.

As we journey through this chapter, we will explore the importance of nature for a child's development, how to prepare for your first forest bathing experience with children, engaging activities to enhance the experience, and ways to nurture mindfulness and respect for nature in children. We will delve into the transformative impact of regular forest bathing on children and how it can foster a lifelong bond with nature.

So, let us embark on this journey, hand in hand with our children, and step into the tranquil embrace of the forest. Let us introduce them to the joy of forest bathing and cultivate a love for nature that will nourish their souls and enrich their lives.

The Importance of Nature for a Child's Development

In the gentle hush of the forest, where sunlight filters through the canopy and the air is imbued with the scent of earth and leaves, a child's development finds a nurturing cradle. In its raw and unfiltered form, nature is a profound teacher, a silent guide, and a playground that fosters growth in ways that the confines of concrete walls and digital screens cannot.

The forest, with its myriad of life forms, textures, sounds, and smells, stimulates a child's senses in a holistic and balanced manner. The rustle of leaves underfoot, the whisper of the wind through the trees, the sight of a squirrel darting up a trunk, the feel of bark under tiny fingers, the taste of wild berries - all these experiences awaken and engage a child's senses, fostering a keen awareness of their surroundings.

In the heart of nature, children learn to appreciate the beauty of simplicity. They discover joy in the smallest things - a fallen leaf, a smooth pebble, a bird's song. This appreciation for simplicity cultivates a sense of contentment and gratitude, qualities that are essential for emotional well-being.

The forest also provides a rich platform for cognitive development. Children learn to recognize patterns and sequences in nature, enhancing their problem-solving skills. They develop spatial awareness as they navigate the woods, and their curiosity is piqued as they explore and make discoveries, fostering a love for learning.

Moreover, the forest is where children can experience freedom and autonomy. They can run, climb, hide, and explore at their own pace, in their own way. This freedom to explore and make decisions enhances their self-confidence and decision-making skills.

In the tranquility of the forest, children also learn the art of mindfulness. They learn to be present, listen, observe, and breathe. This mindfulness reduces stress and anxiety and enhances focus and concentration.

Lastly, children develop a deep-rooted respect and love for the environment by spending time in nature. They learn about the delicate balance of ecosystems, the importance of conservation, and the joy of co-existing with other life forms. This understanding fosters a sense of responsibility and stewardship for the earth, shaping them into conscious and caring adults.

The forest is a nurturing ground for a child's physical, cognitive, emotional, and social development. It is a place where children can grow, learn, and flourish most naturally and joyfully.

Preparing for Your First Forest Bathing Experience with Children

As the sun peeks over the horizon, casting a soft, golden glow on the dew-kissed leaves, you find yourself standing at the edge of the forest, your child's hand nestled warmly in your own. The air is crisp and clean, with the scent of damp earth and wildflowers' faint, sweet perfume. This is the moment you've been waiting for: your first forest bathing experience with children.

Preparing for this experience is not merely about packing the right snacks or dressing in suitable attire, though these practicalities are essential. It is about setting the stage for a journey of discovery that will awaken your child's senses, ignite their curiosity, and foster a deep, enduring love for nature.

Begin by choosing a day when you both are free from obligations. Forest bathing is not an activity to be rushed; it is a slow, deliberate immersion into the natural world. Choose a forest that is safe and accessible, but also rich in biodiversity. The more variety in flora and fauna, the more engaging the experience will be for your child.

Before you set foot in the forest, take a moment to explain to your child what forest bathing is. Use simple, clear language that they can understand. You might say, "We're going on a special adventure in the forest today. We're not going to walk fast or try to get anywhere. We're just going to be in the forest, looking, listening, and feeling. It's like taking a bath in the forest, but we're bathing our senses, not our bodies."

Encourage your child to leave their toys and gadgets behind. This is a time for them to engage directly with nature, unmediated by screens or artificial distractions. Instead, equip them with a magnifying glass, a notebook, and colored pencils for drawing what they observe.

Dress appropriately for the weather and the terrain. Comfortable, sturdy shoes are a must, as are clothes that can get a little dirty. After all, the best forest bathing experiences often involve a bit of mud and leaf litter!

Finally, set some ground rules to ensure safety and respect for nature. Remind your child to stay close, to avoid disturbing wildlife, and to leave no trace behind.

As you prepare for this first forest bathing experience with your child, remember that the goal is not to 'do' but to 'be.' It is about being present, being curious, and being open to the wonders that nature has to offer. It is about cultivating a love for nature that will, with hope and care, grow and flourish in your child's heart, just like the mighty trees in the forest you are about to explore.

Engaging Activities to Enhance the Forest Bathing Experience

As the forest unfurls its verdant arms, welcoming you and your little ones into its tranquil embrace, it's time to explore the myriad of engaging activities that can enhance your forest bathing experience. These activities are about keeping children entertained and fostering a deep, meaningful connection with nature that will nourish their souls and ignite their curiosity.

Begin with a simple sensory exploration. Encourage your children to close their eyes and tune into the sounds of the forest. The rustling leaves whispering ancient tales, the bird's distant call, the wind's soft sigh - all these sounds create a soothing melody that can calm the busiest of minds. Ask them to touch a tree's rough bark, feel the coolness of a leaf, or the delicate softness of a mossy patch. Each texture tells a story, and each sensation is a thread in the intricate tapestry of the forest.

Next, engage their sense of smell. The forest is a treasure trove of natural aromas. The earthy scent of the soil, the fresh fragrance of pine needles, the sweet perfume of wildflowers - each inhalation is a step deeper into the heart of the forest. This olfactory exploration enhances their sensory experience and helps them develop a keen awareness of their surroundings.

A scavenger hunt is another delightful activity that can add a dash of adventure to your forest bathing experience. Create a list of natural items for them to find - a feather, a pinecone, a smooth stone, or a leaf of a specific shape. This sharpens their observation skills and encourages them to interact with the forest respectfully and mindfully.

Introduce them to the art of forest journaling. Provide them with a notebook and some colored pencils, and encourage them to sketch what they see, write about their feelings, or jot down the sounds they hear. This practice nurtures their creativity and helps them healthily process their experiences and emotions.

Lastly, engage them in the simple joy of quiet contemplation. Find a comfortable spot, perhaps under the shade of a towering tree or by a babbling brook, and encourage them to sit quietly, observe, breathe, and be. This mindfulness practice, being fully present in the moment, is one of the most precious gifts that forest bathing can offer.

These activities, woven into the fabric of your forest bathing experience, can transform a simple walk in the woods into a magical journey of discovery, learning, and growth. They can help your children cultivate a deep love for nature, a love that will guide them, inspire them, and nourish them throughout their lives.

Nurturing Mindfulness and Respect for Nature in Children

A child can learn to be genuinely present in the heart of the forest, where the air is pure, and the silence is punctuated only by the rustling of leaves and the songs of birds. This is the essence of mindfulness - the ability to fully engage in the here and now, be aware of one's surroundings and appreciate the beauty of the moment. Forest bathing provides an ideal setting for nurturing this quality in children.

Begin by encouraging your child to close their eyes and take a deep breath, inhaling the scent of the forest. Ask them to focus on the sensation of the air entering their lungs, the feeling of the earth beneath their feet, and the sun's warmth on their skin. This simple exercise can help them tune into their senses and become more aware of their connection to the natural world.

Next, invite them to open their eyes and look at the forest around them. Encourage them to notice the different shades of green, the patterns of light and shadow, and how the leaves move in the breeze. Ask them to listen to the sounds of the forest - the rustling of leaves, the chirping of birds, the distant murmur of a stream. This can help them develop a deeper appreciation for the beauty and complexity of nature.

Teaching children to respect nature is another crucial aspect of forest bathing. This can be as simple as reminding them not to litter, to stay on the trails, and to avoid disturbing the wildlife. But it can also involve more profound lessons about the interconnectedness of all living things and the importance of preserving the natural world for future generations.

One effective way to foster this respect is by involving children in conservation activities, such as planting trees or cleaning up litter. This can help them understand that they have a role in protecting the environment and that their actions can make a difference.

In the tranquility of the forest, children can learn to be mindful, to appreciate the beauty of nature, and to respect the environment. These valuable lessons can enrich their lives and help them grow into responsible, caring adults. In the process, they will also discover a lifelong love for nature and a sense of peace and joy they can carry wherever they go.

The Transformative Impact of Regular Forest Bathing on Children

Regular forest bathing, a practice steeped in simplicity and profound impact, can be a transformative experience for children, shaping their relationship with nature and themselves.

The forest is a living, breathing classroom where every leaf, every stone, every creature has a story to tell. As children immerse themselves in this natural wonder, they learn to observe, question, and explore. They learn about the interconnectedness of life, the delicate balance that sustains it, and their role within this grand tapestry. This understanding fosters a sense of responsibility, a respect for nature that transcends the superficial and seeps into their very being.

The forest also teaches children about the rhythms of life, the ebb and flow of seasons, and the cycle of growth and decay. In this ever-changing yet constant environment, children learn to appreciate the beauty of transience, the value of patience, and the virtue of resilience. They learn that, like the forest, they can weather storms and bloom anew.

Moreover, forest bathing is a journey into the self. As children wander amidst the trees, they also navigate the landscape of their emotions, thoughts, and dreams. With its tranquil solitude, the forest provides a safe space for introspection and self-discovery. It encourages children to listen to their inner voice, trust their instincts, and believe in their potential.

The impact of regular forest bathing on children is not just immediate but enduring. It shapes their perspective, their values, and their behavior. It instills in them a love for nature that is not just an interest but a way of life. It equips them with the tools to lead a mindful, balanced, and fulfilling life.

In the end, forest bathing is more than just a walk in the woods. It invites children to embrace the world with open hearts and curious minds. It is a promise of a lifelong bond with nature, a bond that nurtures them, inspires them, and guides them on their journey through life.

Fostering a Lifelong Bond with Nature through Forest Bathing

As the sun sets on our journey through the verdant realm of forest bathing with children, we find ourselves standing at the threshold of a new dawn. A dawn where our children, imbued with a profound love for nature, step forward to become the stewards of our planet. This is the transformative power of forest bathing, a practice that rejuvenates the senses and fosters a lifelong bond with nature.

The forest, with its towering trees, rustling leaves, and the symphony of birdsong, is a living, breathing classroom. Here, children learn the language of the wind, the secrets of the soil, and the stories written in the stars. Each forest bathing experience is a chapter in their lifelong journey of discovery, a journey that nurtures their curiosity, creativity, and compassion.

As we guide our children through this journey, we are not merely teaching them to appreciate the beauty of nature. We are helping them understand their place in the grand tapestry of life. We show them that they are not separate from nature but integral to it. This understanding, this sense of interconnectedness, is the foundation of a deep and enduring love for nature.

Forest bathing is not a one-time event but a continuous process of growth and transformation. Each visit to the forest is an opportunity to deepen our connection with nature, to learn from its wisdom, and to be healed by its tranquility. As our children grow, so too does their bond with the forest. It becomes a sanctuary of peace in a chaotic world, a source of inspiration in times of doubt, and a wellspring of joy in moments of celebration.

In conclusion, forest bathing with children is a journey of the heart, a dance of the soul, and a celebration of life. It is a gift that we give our children, a gift they will carry with them long after they have grown. We plant a seed of love in their hearts, a seed that will grow into a mighty tree deeply rooted in the soil of respect and reverence for nature.

As we step out of the forest, we carry with us the whispers of the wind, the birds' songs, and the earth's fragrance. We carry the memories of shared laughter, wonder, and silence. But most importantly, we promise a brighter future, where our children, bathed in the light of love for nature, lead the way towards a more harmonious and sustainable world.

Chapter Summary

- Forest bathing can be a transformative experience for children, nurturing their physical, emotional, and cognitive development.
- The forest, with its myriad of life forms, textures, sounds, and smells, stimulates a child's senses in a holistic and balanced manner, fostering a keen awareness of their surroundings and a deep-rooted respect and love for the environment.
- Preparing for a forest bathing experience with children involves choosing a suitable day and location, explaining the concept in simple terms, and setting ground rules for safety and respect for nature.
- Engaging in sensory exploration, scavenger hunts, forest journaling, and quiet contemplation can enhance the forest bathing experience, fostering a deep, meaningful connection with nature.
- Forest bathing provides an ideal setting for nurturing mindfulness in children, teaching them to be fully engaged in the here and now, aware of their surroundings, and appreciate the beauty of the moment.
- Regular forest bathing can transform children, shaping their relationship with nature and themselves, fostering a sense of responsibility and respect for nature, and equipping them with the tools to lead a mindful, balanced, and fulfilling life.
- Forest bathing is a continuous process of growth and transformation; each visit to the forest deepens the child's connection with nature, and as they grow, so does their bond with the forest.

- Forest bathing with children is a journey of the heart, a dance of the soul, and a celebration of life. It is a gift that we give to our children, a gift that they will carry with them long after they have grown, deeply rooted in the soil of respect and reverence for nature.

9

FOREST BATHING IN URBAN SPACES: FINDING YOUR GREEN OASIS

T he quest for green can seem daunting in the heart of the city, where steel and concrete reign supreme. The urban landscape, with its towering skyscrapers and bustling streets, often leaves little room for the tranquil embrace of nature. Yet, amidst the relentless hum of city life, there exists a quiet yearning for the soothing whispers of the wind, the gentle rustle of leaves, and the calming rhythm of life that pulses in the forest's heart. This is the quest for green in the concrete jungle, a journey towards finding your oasis of tranquility amidst the urban chaos.

For all its vibrancy and dynamism, the city can often feel overwhelming. The constant rush, the ceaseless noise, and the ever-present pressure can take a toll on the most resilient spirits. In such times, the soul seeks solace, a place of quiet where one can reconnect with oneself and the world around. This is where the concept of forest bathing comes into play.

Forest bathing is not about hiking or jogging through a forest. It is about immersing oneself in the forest atmosphere, about letting the forest in. It is about taking the time to slow down, breathe in the fresh air, listen to the subtle symphony of nature, and let the forest cleanse your mind and rejuvenate your spirit.

But how does one embark on this journey of forest bathing in the heart of the city? How does one find a green oasis amidst the concrete and steel? This chapter aims to guide you on this journey, to help you discover your own urban green spaces where you can practice forest bathing and find a moment of peace amidst the urban hustle.

The quest for green in the concrete jungle is not just a journey toward finding a physical space. It is a journey towards finding a state of mind, peace, and tranquility that comes from being in harmony with nature, even in the most unlikely places. It is about finding a way to bring the forest to the city, creating a space where the soul can breathe freely, the mind can find respite, and the spirit can soar.

So, let us embark on this journey together. Let us explore the concept of urban forest bathing and discover how to find our own green oasis in the heart of the concrete jungle.

Urban Forest Bathing: A Breath of Fresh Air

In the heart of the city, where steel and concrete reign supreme, the concept of forest bathing may seem like a distant dream, a luxury reserved for those who can escape to the countryside. Yet, the essence of forest bathing is not confined to the wilderness. It is a practice that can be embraced anywhere, even amidst the urban sprawl.

Urban forest bathing is the art of finding tranquility and rejuvenation in our cities' green spaces. It is about immersing oneself in the presence of trees, plants, and the open sky, even if skyscrapers surround them. It is about seeking solace in the rustle of leaves, the chirping of birds, the whisper of the wind, and the dance of sunlight through the foliage, all within the confines of the city.

This concept is not about the size of the green space or the number of trees it houses. It is about the quality of the connection that one can forge with nature in these spaces. A single tree in a busy street, a small park tucked away in a residential area, a rooftop garden, or even a balcony filled with potted plants can serve as an oasis for urban forest bathing.

Urban forest bathing is a reminder that nature is not separate from us but exists only in remote locations. It is all around us, even in the most urbanized settings. It is a call to slow down, breathe, observe, and connect with the natural world amid our hectic city lives.

The concept of urban forest bathing is a breath of fresh air because it offers a way to experience the healing power of nature without leaving the city. It is a practice that can be woven into the fabric of our daily lives, a practice that can make our cities feel a little less grey and a little more green. It is a practice that can help us find balance, peace, and rejuvenation, even in the heart of the concrete jungle.

Identifying Potential Green Oases: Your Urban Forest Bathing Spots

The quest for a green oasis might seem daunting in the heart of the city, where steel and concrete dominate the landscape. Yet, even in the most urbanized environments, nature persists, carving out pockets of tranquility amidst the hustle and bustle. These are your potential urban forest bathing spots, your green oases, waiting to be discovered and cherished.

Begin your search by opening your senses to the world around you. Listen for the rustle of leaves, the chirping of birds, the whisper of wind through the branches. Look for the subtle shades of green that break the monotony of the cityscape. Smell the earthy scent of soil after a rain, the sweet fragrance of blooming flowers, and the fresh aroma of dew-kissed grass. Feel the rough bark of a tree, the softness of moss, the coolness of a leaf's shade. Taste the crispness of the air after a storm, the sweetness of a ripe berry, the tang of a leaf's sap.

Parks are the most obvious choice for urban forest bathing. They are designed to be green spaces where nature is nurtured and protected. Seek out the quiet corners, the secluded spots, the areas where the trees grow thick, and the grass runs wild.

But don't limit yourself to parks. Look for other green spaces that might be overlooked. A tree-lined street, a rooftop garden, a courtyard filled with plants, and a riverbank teeming with life can all serve as your urban forest bathing spots.

Community gardens are another excellent option. They are green spaces and social spaces where you can connect with others who share your love for nature. Participating in a community garden can deepen your forest bathing experience, adding a layer of community and camaraderie to the tranquility and rejuvenation.

Even the smallest patch of green can serve as an urban forest bathing spot. A single tree can be a source of calm and comfort, a place to rest and recharge. A cluster of potted plants can be a mini forest, a tiny oasis in the concrete desert.

Remember, the goal of forest bathing is not to find the most spectacular or pristine natural setting but to connect with nature deeply and meaningfully. Even in the city's heart, you can find your green oasis, your sanctuary of serenity and peace. So, step out of your door, open your senses, and let the city reveal its hidden green treasures.

Techniques for Forest Bathing in Urban Spaces

Even amidst the grey, there are pockets of green waiting to be discovered and bathed in. Forest bathing in urban spaces is not just possible; it is a necessity, a balm for the weary urban soul. Here, we delve into the techniques to help you embrace the green amidst the grey.

The first step is to find your green oasis. It could be a park, a community garden, a tree-lined street, or even a balcony filled with potted plants. The size of the space does not matter as much as the quality of your engagement with it. Once you have found your green oasis, make it a point to visit it regularly. The more familiar you become with the space, the deeper your connection will be.

When you step into your green oasis, leave behind the hustle and bustle of the city. Leave behind your worries, your to-do lists, and your deadlines. This is a time for you to be present and in the moment. As you enter the space, take a deep breath. Let the air fill your lungs; let the scent of the greenery fill your senses. This is the beginning of your urban forest bathing experience.

Walk slowly, mindfully. Feel the ground beneath your feet, the breeze on your skin. Listen to the rustle of the leaves, the birds chirping, and the insects' hum. Look at the different shades of green, the patterns of the leaves, and how the sunlight filters through the branches. Touch the bark of the trees, the petals of the flowers, and the grass blades. Each of these actions helps you connect with nature and helps you immerse yourself in the experience.

As you walk, practice mindful breathing. Inhale deeply, exhale slowly. With each breath, imagine that you are drawing in the energy of the forest, the vitality of the green. With each exhale, imagine that you are releasing stress and negativity. This is not just a physical exercise. It is a spiritual one, a way of cleansing your spirit, of rejuvenating your soul.

Remember, there is no right or wrong way to forest bathe. The most important thing is to be open and receptive. Let nature guide you; let your instincts guide you. You may find that you are drawn to a particular tree or spot. Follow that instinct. Sit under the tree, lie on the grass, close your eyes, and let your mind wander. This is your time, your space, your moment of tranquility amidst the chaos of the city.

Forest bathing in urban spaces is not just about finding a green oasis. It is about creating one within yourself. It is about finding peace, balance, and belonging in an overwhelming world. So, embrace the green amidst the grey, immerse yourself in the experience, and let the forest bathe you in its healing, rejuvenating energy.

Case Studies: Urban Forest Bathing Experiences

In the city's heart, where the hum of traffic is a constant companion, and skyscrapers reach for the heavens, it may seem impossible to find a tranquil, green oasis. Yet, many have found such spaces and successfully embraced the practice of forest bathing within them. Let us delve into the experiences of these urban dwellers, who have discovered the art of finding serenity amidst the city's chaos.

Case Study 1

Our first case study takes us to the bustling city of New York, where the iconic Central Park serves as a green lung amidst the concrete landscape. Here, we meet Anna, a corporate lawyer who has made forest bathing a part of her daily routine. Before the city fully awakens every morning, she walks on the dew-kissed grass, allowing the cool sensation to seep into her being. She breathes in the fresh air, subtly scented with the earthy aroma of damp soil and the sweet fragrance of blooming flowers. Anna shares that this practice has reduced her stress levels and made her more mindful and appreciative of the natural beauty that exists even in the heart of the city.

Case Study 2

Next, we travel to Tokyo, the city that gave birth to the concept of forest bathing or 'Shinrin-yoku.' Amidst the neon lights and towering buildings, we find the tranquil Meiji Shrine forest. Here, we meet Takana, a tech entrepreneur who has found solace in this urban forest's dense, verdant foliage. He spends his weekends here, immersing himself in the sounds of rustling leaves, chirping birds, and the sight of sunlight filtering through the canopy. Takana believes that forest bathing has improved his mental health and inspired creativity in his work.

Case Study 3

Our final case study brings us to London, where the sprawling Hyde Park offers a green retreat to city dwellers. Here, we meet Emma, a university student who has found a unique way to combine her studies with forest bathing. She often sits by the Serpentine Lake, reading amidst the gentle rustle of leaves and the soft lapping of water against the shore. Emma shares that this practice has helped her focus better on her studies and instilled a deep sense of calm and peace.

~

These stories testify to the transformative power of forest bathing, even in the most unlikely places. They remind us that nature is not confined to remote forests or mountain tops but can be found in the heart of our cities, waiting to offer us a moment of tranquility and rejuvenation.

The Impact of Urban Forest Bathing

In the city's heart, where the hum of traffic and the rhythm of urban life are constant companions, forest bathing may seem like a distant dream. Yet, as we have explored, engaging in this practice within the confines of our urban landscapes is not only possible but also profoundly beneficial. The impact of urban forest bathing, both on a personal and environmental level, is a testament to the resilience of nature and the human spirit's innate connection to it.

On a personal level, urban forest bathing offers a sanctuary of serenity amidst the urban chaos. It is a gentle reminder that tranquility can be found even in the most unexpected places. The rustle of leaves underfoot, the dappled sunlight filtering through the branches, the scent of damp earth after a rain shower - these sensory experiences serve as a balm for the weary urban soul. They ground us, reminding us of our inherent connection to the natural world, a connection often forgotten in the hustle and bustle of city life.

Forest bathing in urban spaces also fosters mindfulness, a state of being fully present and engaged in the current moment. As we navigate the green oases within our concrete jungles, we become more attuned to the subtle changes in our environment - the shifting patterns of light and shadow, the changing seasons reflected in the foliage, and the quiet inhabitants of these urban forests. This heightened awareness extends beyond our forest bathing sessions, influencing our daily interactions and experiences.

From an environmental perspective, urban forest bathing underscores the importance of preserving and nurturing green spaces within our cities. These green oases serve as vital lungs for our urban environments, absorbing carbon dioxide, filtering pollutants, and providing a habitat for various flora and fauna. They are a testament to the resilience of nature, flourishing amidst concrete and steel.

Moreover, as more individuals engage in urban forest bathing, there is a growing recognition of the value of these green spaces. This awareness can translate into action, inspiring urban planning policies that prioritize creating and preserving green spaces. It can also foster a sense of community stewardship, encouraging city dwellers to care for their local green oases actively.

In conclusion, the impact of urban forest bathing is far-reaching, touching both the personal and environmental spheres. It is a practice that nurtures the human spirit, fosters mindfulness, and promotes environmental stewardship. As we continue to navigate the complexities of urban life, these green oases remind us of the tranquility and rejuvenation that nature offers, even in the heart of the concrete jungle.

The Future of Forest Bathing in Urban Spaces

As our journey through the verdant labyrinth of urban forest bathing draws close, we find ourselves standing on the precipice of a future where the green and the grey coexist in harmonious balance. The future of forest bathing in urban spaces is not a distant dream but a tangible reality slowly unfurling its emerald tendrils in the heart of our concrete jungles.

The cityscape, often perceived as a monotonous expanse of steel and stone, is gradually reimagined as a canvas where the vibrant strokes of nature can be artfully woven into the urban fabric. Forest bathing in urban spaces is gaining momentum, not just as a wellness trend but as a transformative lifestyle that encourages a deeper connection with the natural world, even within the confines of our bustling metropolises.

As we move forward, the potential for urban forest bathing is immense. The green oases we have identified and explored can multiply, sprouting in every corner of our cities, from the smallest pocket parks to the expansive urban forests. These spaces can serve as sanctuaries where city dwellers can retreat to immerse themselves in the soothing balm of nature, breathe in the verdant air, and let the tranquility of the forest seep into their beings.

The techniques we have discussed for forest bathing in urban spaces will continue to evolve, adapting to each city's unique challenges and opportunities. The experiences shared in our case studies serve as a testament to the transformative power of urban forest bathing, and we hope that they inspire countless more such experiences.

From a personal perspective, urban forest bathing can become vital for stress management, mental clarity, and overall well-being. From an environmental perspective, the rise of urban forest bathing can foster a greater appreciation for our urban green spaces, leading to more concerted conservation efforts and sustainable urban planning.

In conclusion, the future of forest bathing in urban spaces is a vision of cities where the green and the grey dance in a harmonious ballet, where the rustle of leaves is a familiar soundtrack, and where every city dweller can experience the profound tranquility of forest bathing. It is a future where our cities are not just habitats but sanctuaries of well-being, where the healing power of nature is just a few steps away, waiting to be discovered in our green oases.

Chapter Summary

- The quest for green in the concrete jungle is a journey toward finding tranquility amidst urban chaos. This is achieved through forest bathing, which involves immersing oneself in the forest atmosphere to rejuvenate the spirit.
- Urban forest bathing is the art of finding tranquility in the green spaces within cities. It involves seeking solace in the presence of trees, plants, and the open sky, even if surrounded by skyscrapers.
- Identifying potential green oases in the city involves opening your senses to the world. Parks, tree-lined streets, rooftop gardens, courtyards filled with plants, and riverbanks teeming with life can all serve as urban forest bathing spots.
- Techniques for forest bathing in urban spaces involve finding and visiting a green oasis regularly, walking slowly and mindfully, practicing mindful breathing, and allowing nature and your instincts to guide you.
- The impact of urban forest bathing is profound on both a personal and environmental level. It offers a sanctuary of serenity, fosters mindfulness, underscores the importance of

preserving green spaces, and promotes environmental stewardship.

- The future of forest bathing in urban spaces is promising. The concept is gaining momentum and has the potential to transform cities into sanctuaries of well-being where the healing power of nature is accessible to all city dwellers.
- Urban forest bathing can improve stress management, mental clarity, and well-being. It can also foster a greater appreciation for urban green spaces, leading to more concerted conservation efforts and sustainable urban planning.

10

TRANSFORMATIVE EXPERIENCES OF FOREST BATHING

In its timeless wisdom, the forest offers a gentle refuge from the clamor of our daily lives. It is a testament to resilience and growth, its towering trees reaching the sky in a silent symphony of life. Here, amidst the rustling leaves and the soft hum of life, we find a space to reconnect with our inner selves, heal, and rejuvenate.

Forest bathing is an intimate communion with nature, a mindful immersion into the forest's soothing balm. It is a practice that encourages us to slow down, listen to the whispers of the wind, feel the cool touch of moss under our fingertips, and gaze upon the intricate patterns of leaves and bark. In these moments of quiet contemplation, we begin to understand the profound healing power of the forest.

The anecdotes that follow in this chapter illustrate experiences you may encounter in your forest bathing journey, as well as narratives of individuals who have experienced the transformative power of forest bathing. They speak of awakenings and profound revelations, sensory experiences that have stirred souls, and the lasting impressions the forest has left upon hearts. These are experiences of renewal and transformation, the resurgence of hope, and the enduring call of the forest.

As you journey through these narratives, may you find inspiration and solace in the experiences of others. May you step into the forest's healing embrace, breathe in its tranquility, and allow its energy to rejuve-nate your spirit. For in the heart of the forest, there is a serenity waiting to welcome you, a sanctuary where you can find healing, peace, and a profound connection with the natural world.

The Awakening: A First Encounter with Forest Bathing

The story begins with awakening in the forest's heart, where the sunlight filters through the verdant canopy, casting dappled shadows on the forest floor. It is a tale not of grand adventures or epic quests but of a quiet, profound encounter with the natural world. It is the story of the first experience of forest bathing.

Imagine stepping into the forest, leaving behind the clamor of the everyday world. The air is cool and fresh, filled with the scent of damp earth and the subtle perfume of wildflowers. The only sounds are the rustling of leaves in the breeze, the distant call of a bird, and the soft crunch of your footsteps on the forest floor. It is a world apart, a sanc-tuary of tranquility and peace.

As you walk deeper into the forest, you feel a sense of calm washing over you. The worries and stresses of life seem to fall away, replaced by a feeling of serenity and contentment. You are not merely in the forest; you are a part of it, connected to it profoundly and intimately.

You begin to notice things you might have overlooked before: the intricate patterns of bark on a tree trunk, the delicate beauty of a single leaf, and the way the light dances on the surface of a stream. You feel the coolness of the earth beneath your feet, the sun's warmth on your skin, and the gentle caress of the breeze. You breathe deeply, filling your lungs with pure, clean air.

This is the awakening, the first encounter with forest bathing. It is a moment of revelation, a realization of the deep connection between your-self and the natural world. It is a feeling of being fully present, fully alive, fully human.

At this moment, you understand what it means to bathe in the forest, to immerse yourself in nature, to let it wash over you and cleanse you, body and soul. You feel a sense of peace and tranquility you have never known before, a sense of being at one with the world around you.

This is the beginning of a journey of discovery and transformation. It is a journey that will take you deeper into the heart of the forest and the heart of yourself. It is a journey that begins with a single step, breath, and moment of awakening.

The Journey Within: Profound Revelations Amidst the Trees

The forest is a stage for the journey within, a transformative process that unfolds as one immerses oneself in the serene embrace of the forest.

The journey begins with a single step: a conscious decision to leave behind the clamor of the outside world and step into the tranquil realm of the forest. As the forest bathers recounted, this initial step was often accompanied by a sense of trepidation, a fear of the unknown. Yet, as they ventured deeper into the forest, this fear gradually gave way to a sense of peace and tranquility.

With its timeless wisdom, the forest has a way of peeling back the layers of our consciousness, revealing the core of our being. Amidst the towering trees and the gentle rustle of leaves, bathers confronted their deepest fears, unfulfilled dreams, and most cherished hopes. In its silent eloquence, the forest provided a safe space for these revelations to surface, allowing the bathers to acknowledge and confront these hidden aspects of themselves.

One bather recounted how, in the serenity of the forest, she found the courage to face a painful memory that she had long suppressed. As she sat beneath a towering pine, she felt a surge of emotion well up within her. She allowed herself to feel the pain, cry, and eventually let go. In its infinite compassion, the forest bore witness to her pain and provided solace in its tranquil embrace.

Another bather spoke of a profound realization that dawned upon him as he watched a leaf gently fall to the ground. He realized the impermanence of life and the importance of living in the present moment. This revelation, he shared, transformed his perspective on life and instilled a deep sense of peace.

These stories of profound revelations amidst the trees testify to the transformative power of forest bathing. With its serene beauty and timeless wisdom, the forest invites us on a journey that leads to self-discovery, healing, and transformation. As we immerse ourselves in the tranquil embrace of the forest, we embark on a journey of self-discovery that leads us back to our true selves.

The Symphony of Nature: Sensory Experiences in Forest Bathing

In the heart of the forest, a symphony of nature unfolds. The concert requires no ticket, no grand hall, only an open heart and a willingness to listen. The forest is a maestro, conducting a harmonious orchestra of sights, sounds, scents, and sensations that awaken the senses and soothe the soul.

Imagine standing amidst the towering trees, their leaves whispering secrets in the gentle breeze. The rustle of foliage is a soft lullaby, a soothing serenade that invites you to let go of your worries and surrender to the rhythm of nature. The forest floor, a carpet of moss and fallen leaves, crunches softly underfoot, a tactile reminder of the life beneath the surface.

The air is alive with pine and damp earth, a heady perfume that fills the lungs and cleanses the spirit. The forest is a sensory feast, a banquet of natural wonders that nourishes the soul. Each breath is a sip of pure, unfiltered air, each step a taste of nature's wild, untamed beauty.

The forest is a canvas of colors, a masterpiece painted by the hand of Mother Nature. The vibrant green of the leaves, the rich brown of the bark, the delicate hues of wildflowers that dot the landscape - each detail is a brushstroke in this breathtaking tableau. The sunlight filters through the canopy, casting dappled shadows that dance and play on the forest floor.

And then there are the sounds - the chirping of birds, the rustling of leaves, the distant murmur of a babbling brook. Each note is a part of the forest's symphony, a melody that resonates in the heart and echoes in the soul.

Forest bathing is not merely a walk in the woods. It is an immersive experience, a sensory journey that invites you to connect profoundly with nature. It is a symphony of nature, a concert that plays on the soul's strings and leaves a melody that lingers long after the forest fades from view.

In the embrace of the forest, we find a sanctuary, a place of peace and tranquility where the symphony of nature plays on an endless loop. It is here, amidst the trees, that we find ourselves, our senses awakened, our spirits rejuvenated. The forest is not just a place but a state of being, a symphony that plays in the heart of every forest bather.

The Resurgence: Stories of Renewal and Transformation

In the heart of the forest, where the air is thick with the scent of pine and the whispers of the wind, a profound resurgence occurs. It is a rebirth, a renewal, a transformation that is as tangible as the bark of the trees and as ethereal as the dappled sunlight filtering through the leaves.

One such story of resurgence is that of Maria, a woman who found herself lost in the labyrinth of life. She was trapped in the relentless pace of the modern world, her spirit dulled by the monotony of routine. It was in the forest that Maria found her way back to herself. As she immersed herself in the verdant embrace of the trees, she felt a shift within her. With its timeless wisdom and tranquil beauty, the forest began to heal her. She felt her worries seeping away into the earth beneath her feet, replaced by a sense of peace she had long forgotten.

Then, there was John, a man who weathered the storms of life. He carried the weight of loss and grief, his heart heavy with sorrow. It was in the forest that John found solace. The gentle rustling of the leaves, the soft murmur of the brook, and the quiet hum of life all around him all spoke to his aching heart. He found comfort in the forest's silent companionship, its quiet understanding. In its infinite patience, the forest allowed him to grieve, heal, and grow.

And so, these stories of resurgence continue, each unique, each profound. They are stories of individuals touched by the healing power of the forest, their lives forever changed. They speak of the transformative experiences of forest bathing, of the renewal and transformation that takes place in its serene depths.

In the forest, the spirit is resurgent, rekindling the soul. It is a place where one can shed the burdens of the past and embrace the promise of the future. It is a place of renewal, of transformation, of resurgence. In these personal stories, we see the true power of forest bathing and the profound impact it can have on our lives.

As we journey deeper into the forest, we continue to uncover these stories, these echoes of resurgence. They are a testament to the enduring call of the forest, a call that resonates within us all.

The Echoes of the Forest: Lasting Impressions of Forest Bathing

In the tranquility of the forest, where the whispers of the wind converse with the rustling leaves, where the sunbeams filter through the verdant canopy to kiss the earth below, there is a profound connection to be made. This connection, once established, leaves an indelible imprint on the soul, a lasting impression that echoes long after one has left the forest's embrace.

These echoes of the forest are not merely memories of a place visited or an activity undertaken. They are the resonances of a deep, transformative experience, a communion with nature that transcends the boundaries of the physical world. They are the silent reminders of the forest's healing power, the gentle nudges towards introspection and self-discovery, and the subtle prompts to slow down, breathe, and be.

Each echo is unique, as unique as the individual who carries it. For some, the memory of the forest's tranquility and the serenity enveloped them as they bathed in the forest's atmosphere. It is the recollection of the soft rustle of leaves underfoot, the soothing murmur of a distant stream, the gentle caress of the wind. The remembrance of a profound peace seemed to seep into their very bones, calming their minds, easing their worries, and filling their hearts with quiet joy.

For others, the echo is a sensory memory, a vivid recall of the forest's sights, sounds, and scents. It is the memory of the vibrant foliage greens, the dappled sunlight on the forest floor, and the sudden flash of a bird in flight. It is the recollection of the forest's symphony, the harmonious blend of bird calls, rustling leaves, and the soft sigh of the wind. It is the remembrance of the forest's scent, the earthy aroma of damp soil, the fresh fragrance of leaves, and the subtle perfume of wildflowers.

Yet for others, the echo is a spiritual resonance, a lingering connection with the natural world. It is the memory of a profound sense of belonging, of feeling at one with the forest, tree, leaf, and creature. It is the recollection of a deep sense of awe and wonder, a humbling realization of the grandeur of nature and one's small place within it. It is the remembrance of a profound sense of gratitude, a heartfelt thankfulness for the healing, the peace, and the joy that the forest bathing experience brought.

These echoes of the forest, these lasting impressions, serve as gentle reminders of the transformative power of forest bathing. They are the silent testimonies of the healing embrace of the forest, the quiet affirmations of the profound connections made, and the subtle invitations to return to bathe once more in the forest's tranquil, immersive, and rejuvenating atmosphere. They are the enduring call of the forest, a call that resonates within the heart and is impossible to ignore once heard.

The Enduring Call of the Forest

As our journey through the leafy heart of the forest draws to a close, we find ourselves standing on the threshold of a profound understanding. The enduring call of the forest, a siren song that resonates deep within our souls, is not merely an invitation to step into a world of tranquility and beauty. It is a gentle summons to return to our roots, to reconnect with the primal essence of our being, and to rediscover the healing power of nature that lies dormant within us.

In its timeless wisdom, the forest has whispered its secrets into our hearts. It has shown us that we are not separate from the natural world but an integral part of it. We have breathed in its life-giving air, bathed in its dappled sunlight, and listened to its symphony of sounds. We have felt the earth's pulse beneath our feet and the wind's caress on our skin. We have tasted the sweetness of its fruits and drank from its crystal-clear streams. In these moments of profound connection, we have experienced a sense of peace and well-being that transcends the physical realm, touching the very core of our being.

The transformative experiences of forest bathing are not fleeting moments of bliss but lasting impressions that continue to shape our lives long after we have left the forest. They awaken a deep reverence for nature, a heightened awareness of our surroundings, and a renewed sense of purpose. They inspire us to live more mindfully, to tread more lightly on the earth, and to cherish the precious gift of life.

As we step out of the forest and back into the hustle and bustle of our daily lives, we carry the echoes of the forest with us. We remember the rustle of the leaves, the bird's song, the flowers' fragrance, and the air's stillness. We remember feeling fully present, fully alive, and fully connected to the world around us. And we yearn to return to the forest, bathe once again in its healing embrace, and answer the wild's enduring call.

In the end, forest bathing is more than a practice. It is a way of life, a path to wellness, and a journey of self-discovery. It is a reminder that we are part of a larger whole, a testament to the healing power of nature, and a celebration of the beauty and wonder of the world we inhabit. It is, in essence, a return to the source, a homecoming to the heart of the forest, and a reawakening to the magic and mystery of life itself.

Chapter Summary

- Forest bathing is a practice that invites us to immerse ourselves in nature, allowing its tranquil energy to permeate our being, offering a sanctuary of serenity and healing.
- The first encounter with forest bathing is often a profound awakening, a realization of the deep connection between oneself and the natural world, leading to peace and tranquility.
- The forest invites introspection and self-discovery, providing a safe space for individuals to confront their deepest fears,

unfulfilled dreams, and cherished hopes, leading to profound revelations and transformations.

- Forest bathing is an immersive sensory experience, a symphony of nature that awakens the senses and soothes the soul, connecting individuals with nature on a profound level.
- The forest provides a space for a resurgence of the spirit, a rekindling of the soul, where individuals can shed burdens and embrace the promise of the future, leading to stories of renewal and transformation.
- The connection with the forest leaves an indelible imprint on the soul, a lasting impression that echoes long after one has left the forest's embrace, as a reminder of the transformative power of forest bathing.
- The transformative experiences of forest bathing are not fleeting moments of bliss but lasting impressions that continue to shape our lives long after we have left the forest, inspiring us to live more mindfully and cherish the precious gift of life.
- Forest bathing is more than a practice; it is a way of life, a path to wellness, and a journey of self-discovery, reminding us that we are part of a larger whole and celebrating the beauty and wonder of our world.

YOUR CONTINUED JOURNEY INTO THE FOREST'S EMBRACE

As we stand on the precipice of our concluding chapter, let us pause momentarily, like a leaf suspended in the air before it gently descends to the forest floor. We have journeyed together through the heart of the forest, immersing ourselves in its tranquil embrace, and now it is time to reflect on the path we have trodden.

In its infinite wisdom, the forest has been our guide and sanctuary. It has whispered ancient secrets in our ears, secrets that have been carried on the wind, rustling through the leaves and echoing in the peaceful silence of the woodland. We have learned to listen, to listen, to the forest's whisper indeed, and in doing so, we have discovered a profound connection to the natural world and ourselves.

Our journey into forest bathing has been more than just a walk in the woods. It has been a transformative experience, a gentle immersion into the healing power of nature. We bathed in the dappled sunlight filtering through the canopy, breathed in the earthy scent of the forest floor, and felt the cool touch of the breeze on our skin. We have learned to slow down, to be present, and to open our senses to the subtle symphony of the forest.

As we reflect on our journey, we realize that each step we took, each leaf we touched, and each breath we drew in the forest's embrace has left an indelible imprint on our hearts. We have not merely observed the forest; we have become a part of it, and it has become a part of us.

The forest has taught us to see beauty in simplicity, to find peace in silence, and to draw strength from our roots. It has shown us that we are not separate from nature but intrinsically connected to it. It has reminded us of the importance of balance, giving and receiving, growth and decay, light and shadow.

As we stand here, at the end of our journey, we are not the same as we were at the beginning. We have been touched by the forest's whisper, bathed in its healing light, and transformed by its wisdom. We carry the forest within us, and it continues to guide us, to heal us, and to inspire us.

So, let us take a moment to reflect on our journey, honor the wisdom we have gained, and express our gratitude to the forest for its generous gifts. As we turn the last leaf of our journey, let us carry the forest's whisper in our hearts and let it guide us on our continued journey into the embrace of nature.

The Forest's Whisper: Unveiling the Core Insights

As we stand on the threshold of the forest, the whispering leaves beckon us to delve deeper into the heart of our journey. The soft, soothing melody of the forest's whisper has been our guide, leading us through the verdant labyrinth of self-discovery and tranquility. Here, in the stillness of the forest's embrace, we have unearthed the core insights of our journey, the major themes, and the findings that have shaped our understanding of forest bathing.

The Forest and Our Well-being

The first theme that emerged was the profound connection between the forest and our well-being. The forest, with its lush canopy and vibrant undergrowth, is not merely a backdrop to our lives but an active participant in our journey toward wellness. The rustling leaves, the chirping birds, the gentle sway of the trees - each element of the forest contributes to a symphony of serenity that calms our minds, soothes our souls and rejuvenates our bodies. Forest bathing is not a mere walk in the woods but an immersive experience that engages all our senses, fostering a deep, holistic connection with nature.

Mindfulness

The second theme that surfaced was the transformative power of mindfulness. Forest bathing is not a passive act but an active engagement with the present moment. It invites us to shed the weight of our worries, let go of our preoccupations, and fully immerse ourselves in the here and now. The forest, with its timeless beauty and tranquil rhythm, serves as a mirror, reflecting our inner state of being. As we attune ourselves to the forest's rhythm, we cultivate mindfulness, a heightened awareness, and presence that transforms our perception of self and the world around us.

Healing Power of the Forest

The third theme that emerged was the universality of the forest's healing touch. Forest bathing is not bound by culture, age, or geography. The forest's embrace is a universal sanctuary, a haven of tranquility that welcomes all seeking solace. Whether it is the towering redwoods of California, the ancient cedars of Japan, or the lush rainforests of Brazil, the healing power of the forest transcends boundaries, offering a shared experience of rejuvenation and renewal.

~

As we unveil these core insights, we begin to understand the forest's whisper, the subtle yet profound message that it imparts. The forest, in its tranquil majesty, invites us to reconnect with our true selves, cultivate mindfulness, and experience the universal healing power of nature. It is a whisper that echoes in the rustling leaves, the chirping birds, and the gentle sway of the trees, guiding us on our continued journey into the forest's embrace.

The Ripple in the Pond: The Far-reaching Impact of Forest Bathing

As we stand on the forest's edge, gazing into the verdant depths, we are not merely observers but participants in a grand, interconnected dance of life. Forest bathing, as we have journeyed through it, is not an isolated act but a ripple in the pond of our existence, sending out waves of influence that touch every aspect of our lives.

The implications of forest bathing are as vast and varied as the forest itself. It is not merely a practice of relaxation but a profound reconnection with the natural world, a rekindling of our primal bond with the earth. It is a gentle reminder of our place in the grand tapestry of life, a humbling experience that fosters a deep gratitude and respect for the natural world.

The significance of forest bathing extends beyond the individual, reaching into the societal and environmental realms. As we immerse ourselves in the forest's embrace, we are nurturing our well-being and contributing to the health of our communities and the planet. By fostering a deeper connection with nature, we are more likely to care for it, protect it, and advocate for its preservation.

The ripple effect of forest bathing is also evident in its potential to transform our relationship with technology. In an age where screens and devices often dominate our lives, forest bathing offers a much-needed respite, a chance to unplug and recharge in the most natural way possible. It is a gentle nudge towards balance, a reminder of the simple, profound joy of being present in the moment, of truly seeing, hearing, and feeling the world around us.

The forest's whisper is not a solitary voice but a chorus of wisdom, a symphony of insights that resonate far beyond the forest's edge. As we step out of the forest, we carry these lessons with us, spreading the ripple of forest bathing into our daily lives, communities, and the world. The forest's embrace is not a fleeting experience but a lasting imprint, a gentle guide on our continued journey through life.

The Unseen Trail: Addressing Shortcomings and Counterarguments

As we tread the unseen trail, let us pause to acknowledge the limitations and critiques that have emerged along our journey into the forest's embrace. Like the forest itself, the practice of forest bathing is not without its shadows, hidden corners, and unexplored territories.

The first critique often voiced is the lack of empirical evidence supporting the benefits of forest bathing. While numerous studies have suggested a correlation between time spent in nature and improved mental and physical health, the exact mechanisms behind these effects remain largely uncharted. The forest's whisper speaks in a language that science is still learning to decipher.

Another critique lies in the accessibility of forest bathing. Only some have the privilege of living near expansive, untouched woodlands. Urban dwellers, in particular, may find it challenging to immerse themselves in a forest environment regularly. The forest's embrace, it seems, is not universally accessible.

Furthermore, there is the critique of forest bathing being a solitary activity, potentially leading to feelings of isolation or loneliness. While the forest can provide a sanctuary for solitude, it is not inherently solitary. The rustle of leaves, the chirping of birds, and the whispering wind remind us that the forest is a community, a symphony of life.

Lastly, there is the critique that forest bathing is a form of escapism, a retreat from the realities and responsibilities of daily life. We must remember that the forest is not a place to escape but a place to return to. It is not a denial of reality but a reconnection with the reality that we are part of nature, not separate from it.

In addressing these critiques, we must not shy away from them but rather, like the forest, grow from them. We must continue to advocate for more research into the benefits of forest bathing, promote the creation of green spaces in urban areas, encourage communal forest bathing experiences, and reframe our understanding of what it means to return to nature.

As we continue our journey into the forest's embrace, let us remember that every path has its unseen trails, and every practice has its limitations. But it is in acknowledging these that we can truly appreciate the depth and breadth of the forest's whisper and continue to grow, like the forest itself, in wisdom and resilience.

The Seed's Promise: Proposing the Path Forward

As we stand on the edge of the forest, and our journey through the verdant realm of forest bathing draws to a close, we find ourselves cradling a seed. This seed, small and unassuming, holds within it a promise. A promise of growth, renewal, and a deeper connection with the natural world surrounding us. It symbolizes the path forward, a path we must choose to tread in our own time and in our own way.

The forest, with its towering trees and whispering leaves, has shared with us its secrets. It has shown us the power of silence, the beauty of simplicity, and the profound peace that comes from simply being. It has taught us to breathe, listen, and see with new eyes. But the forest's lessons do not end at its borders. They continue in the seed we now hold, which we must choose to plant and nurture in our lives.

Planting this seed may mean different things to different people. For some, it may mean committing to spend more time in nature, regularly immersing oneself in the forest's tranquil embrace. For others, it may mean adopting a more mindful approach to life, learning to slow down, breathe, and truly see the world around them. And for others still, it may mean advocating for protecting and preserving our natural spaces, ensuring that future generations can also experience the healing power of the forest.

Whatever form your seed takes, I encourage you to plant it carefully and intentionally. Nurture it with patience and love. Allow it to grow at its own pace, knowing that, like the forest, it will not be rushed. And as it grows, let it transform you. Let it deepen your connection with the natural world, others, and yourself. Let it bring you peace, joy, and a sense of belonging.

As we part ways, I leave you with this final thought. In all its tranquil beauty, the forest is not just a place. It is a state of being. It is a way of moving through the world with grace, mindfulness, and a deep respect for all life. It is a journey that does not end but continues in the seed we now hold. So, as you step forward from the forest's edge, remember the seed's promise. Remember the lessons of the forest. And remember that no matter where you are, you can always return to the forest's embrace.

EARTHING ESSENTIALS

A COMPREHENSIVE GUIDE ON GROUNDING, HARNESSING THE HEALING POWER OF NATURE, AND DEEPENING YOUR CONNECTION WITH THE EARTH

THE CALL OF THE EARTH

Amid our bustling lives, there exists a silent whisper, a gentle call that often goes unnoticed. It is a call not heard through the ears but felt through the skin, the soles of our feet, the palms of our hands. It is a call that resonates in the marrow of our bones, in the deepest recesses of our hearts. This is the Earth's silent whisper, a subtle yet profound dialogue between the planet we inhabit and the beings we are.

The Earth, our home, is not merely a passive stage upon which the drama of life unfolds. It is an active participant, a character in its own right, with its own voice and story to tell. Yet, in our modern, technologically-driven world, we have become deaf to this voice. We have insulated ourselves with concrete and steel, rubber and plastic, and in doing so, we have severed the ancient, primal connection that once bound us to the very ground beneath our feet.

But the Earth continues to whisper, to call out to us. It beckons us to remove our shoes and step barefoot onto the grass, sand, and soil. It invites us to feel the cool dampness of morning dew, the warmth of sun-baked clay, and the rough texture of tree bark. It urges us to remember, reconnect, and ground ourselves again in the natural world.

This book explores that call, a journey into the heart of the Earth's silent whisper. It is an invitation to rekindle our relationship with the

Earth, rediscover nature's healing power, and reclaim our place in the grand tapestry of life. Through the practice of earthing, we will learn to listen to the Earth's whisper, respond to its call, and find our footing on the path toward holistic healing.

The Unseen Connection: Man and Earth

In our existence, there exists an unseen thread, a silent symphony that binds us all. It is a profound, intrinsic connection, yet often overlooked. It is the connection between man and Earth.

Imagine, if you will, standing barefoot on a lush, verdant meadow. Feel the cool, damp grass beneath your feet, the gentle hum of the Earth resonating through your soles. The sun is a warm caress on your skin, the wind a soft whisper in your ear. You are here, in this moment, and part of something much larger than yourself. You are a part of the Earth.

This connection is not merely a poetic metaphor but a tangible, physical reality. Like the Earth, our bodies are composed of myriad elements, each a testament to our shared origins. We are, in essence, children of the Earth, born of her bounty and sustained by her grace.

Yet, in our modern, fast-paced world, we have become disconnected. We have traded the soft embrace of the Earth for the cold, sterile touch of concrete. We have swapped the rhythmic pulse of nature for the relentless hum of machinery. We have lost touch with our roots, and in doing so, we have lost a part of ourselves.

But it is not too late to reclaim this connection, to rekindle this ancient bond. Through the practice of earthing, we can ground ourselves, both physically and spiritually. We can reconnect with the Earth and, in doing so, reconnect with ourselves.

This is the unseen connection between man and Earth. It is a call to return, a call to remember, a call to heal. It is a call that echoes in the silence, a call that resonates in the very core of our being. It is the call of the Earth. And it is a call that we must answer.

Grounding Ourselves: A Journey Towards Holistic Healing

In this book, we will embark on a journey, a pilgrimage of sorts, towards a destination as old as time itself, yet as fresh and invigorating as the morning dew. This journey is not one of miles and landscapes but rather a journey of the spirit, the mind, and the body. It is a journey towards grounding ourselves, reconnecting with the Earth, and holistic healing.

The purpose of this book is to serve as a guide, a beacon of light, illuminating the path towards this profound connection. It is an invitation to step outside, to feel the Earth beneath your feet, to breathe in the air, to bask in the sunlight, and to drink from the well of life that is the Earth. It is an invitation to experience nature's healing power, to rediscover our ancestors' wisdom, and to reclaim our birthright as children of the Earth.

This book has many goals. Firstly, it aims to educate and provide a comprehensive understanding of what earthing is, its scientific basis, and its myriad benefits. It seeks to dispel myths, to challenge misconceptions, and to present the facts in a clear, accessible, and engaging manner.

Secondly, this book aims to inspire and ignite a spark of curiosity, wonder, and reverence for the Earth. It seeks to awaken a sense of belonging, interconnectedness, and responsibility towards the Earth and all its inhabitants.

Lastly, this book aims to empower and provide practical guidance on how to incorporate earthing into your daily life, cultivate a deeper connection with the Earth, and harness its healing power for physical, emotional, and spiritual well-being.

In essence, this book is a call to action, a call to return to our roots, to ground ourselves in the Earth, and to embark on a journey towards holistic healing. It is a call to listen to the Earth's silent whisper, to heed its wisdom, and to honor its gifts. It is a call to embrace the unseen connection between man and Earth and to celebrate the beauty, the mystery, and the magic of this extraordinary relationship.

The Path Ahead: Unfolding the Layers of Earthing

As we embark on this journey together, we will traverse the leafy valleys and towering peaks of the concept of earthing. This book is not merely a collection of words but a pathway that will guide us toward a deeper understanding of our connection with the Earth.

In the following chapters, we will delve into the history of and science behind earthing, exploring the intricate web of energy that binds us to our planet. We will examine the physiological and psychological effects of grounding, shedding light on how this simple act can profoundly change our health and well-being.

We will also explore the spiritual aspects of earthing, delving into the ancient wisdom that has long recognized the Earth's healing power. We will learn from indigenous cultures, whose practices and beliefs have been shaped by a deep reverence for the natural world.

In the latter part of the book, we will turn our attention to practical applications. We will learn how to incorporate earthing into our daily lives, whether in the heart of a bustling city or the quiet solitude of the countryside. We will discover how to create spaces in our homes and workplaces that facilitate grounding and how to make the most of our time in nature.

Finally, we will look to the future, considering the implications of earthing for our society and planet. We will reflect on the potential of grounding to foster a more sustainable, holistic way of life and to bring about a more profound sense of connection and harmony in our world.

This journey will not always be easy. It will challenge us to question our assumptions, step outside our comfort zones, and confront the disconnection that often characterizes our modern lives. But as we navigate this path together, we will find that the rewards are worth the effort. By grounding ourselves, we not only enhance our health and well-being but also contribute to the healing of our planet.

So, let us embark on this journey with open minds and hearts, ready to embrace the call of the Earth.

1

THE CONCEPT OF EARTHING: A COMPREHENSIVE OVERVIEW

In the quiet hum of the natural world, beneath the rustling leaves and the whispering winds, lies a concept as old as Earth itself. It is a concept that has been overlooked, forgotten, and often dismissed in our modern, fast-paced world. Yet, it is a concept that can transform our lives profoundly. This concept is earthing, also known as grounding, and it is the focus of our exploration in this chapter.

At its core, earthing, also known as grounding, is the practice of connecting directly with the Earth's natural electric charge. It is the act of walking barefoot on the grass, sleeping on the ground under the stars, and feeling the Earth's pulse beneath our fingertips. It is a return to our roots, a reconnection with the natural world from which we have become increasingly disconnected. The concept of earthing revolves around the idea that direct contact with the Earth's surface allows for the transfer of electrons from the ground into the body. This natural exchange is believed to promote physiological changes and healing benefits.

The simplicity of earthing lies in its accessibility. It requires no sophisticated equipment, no advanced techniques, only the willingness to step outside and make contact with the natural world. Whether through the soles of your feet, the palms of your hands, or any other part of your body, the connection is made between yourself and the Earth.

The concept of earthing is not new. It is woven into the fabric of many indigenous cultures and traditions. Yet, in our modern world, where technology reigns, and concrete jungles dominate, we have lost touch with this fundamental connection. We have insulated ourselves from the Earth with rubber-soled shoes and high-rise buildings, creating a disconnect that has far-reaching implications for our health and well-being.

In this chapter, we will unearth the concept of earthing, delving into its historical roots and the science that supports it. We will provide an overview of the various techniques and methods of earthing and the myriad health benefits it offers. We will also debunk some of the myths and misconceptions surrounding this practice, providing a comprehensive understanding of what earthing is and how it can be incorporated into our daily lives. Many of these topics will appear in later chapters of the book, allowing you to explore them in more detail.

As we embark on this journey, I hope you will approach the concept of earthing with an open mind and a willing heart, for it is in this openness, in this willingness to reconnect with the Earth, that we can truly begin to understand the healing power of earthing. So, let us begin. Let us unearth the concept of earthing, and in doing so, let us reconnect with the natural world and, ultimately, with ourselves.

The Historical Roots of Earthing

The concept of earthing, though seemingly novel, is deeply rooted in the annals of human history. It is a practice woven into the fabric of our existence, subtly influencing our relationship with the natural world. This section aims to provide an overview of the historical roots of earthing, tracing its origins and evolution over time.

In its most primal form, the concept can be traced back to our ancestors who lived in close communion with nature. They walked barefoot, slept on the ground, and cultivated the Earth with their bare hands. Unbeknownst to them, they practiced earthing, absorbing the Earth's energy and benefiting from its healing properties.

In ancient civilizations, the Earth was revered as a motherly presence, a source of life and healing. In many indigenous cultures around the world, the Earth was revered as a source of life and healing. The Native Americans, for instance, believed in the power of Mother Earth to heal and restore balance. They practiced earthing through their rituals and ceremonies, often involving direct contact with the Earth. Similarly, in the East, the ancient practice of yoga recognized the importance of grounding. Many yoga poses are designed to connect the practitioner with the Earth, promoting a sense of balance and tranquility.

The historical roots of earthing also extend to the realm of science. In the 18th century, the renowned scientist Benjamin Franklin conducted experiments on grounding, exploring its effects on electricity. His work laid the foundation for further research into the science of earthing.

However, as societies evolved and industrialization took hold, our connection with the Earth began to wane. Concrete jungles replaced natural landscapes, and rubber-soled shoes became the norm, severing our direct physical contact with the Earth. The practice of earthing was largely forgotten, relegated to the annals of history.

In recent years, however, there has been a resurgence of interest in earthing. This revival is fueled by a growing body of scientific research highlighting the health benefits of grounding and a broader societal shift towards holistic and naturalistic approaches to well-being.

The historical roots of earthing remind us of our innate connection with the Earth. They invite us to rediscover this connection, to return to our roots, and to embrace earthing as a holistic approach to well-being. As we delve deeper into the science and practice of earthing in the following chapters, let us keep in mind this historical perspective, grounding our understanding in the rich soil of our past.

The Science Behind Earthing: A Closer Look

In the heart of the forest, beneath the vast, azure sky, the Earth pulses with an ancient, natural rhythm. This rhythm, this energy, is not merely a poetic metaphor but a scientific reality that forms the basis of the concept of earthing.

Imagine, if you will, the feeling of walking barefoot on a dewy stretch of grass, the sensation of sand sifting between your toes on a beach, or the solid embrace of rock underfoot on a mountain trail. These experiences are not just tactile pleasures; they are instances of earthing, moments when your body connects with the Earth's surface, tapping into its vast electrical field.

The Earth, you see, is a massive reservoir of negatively charged free electrons. These electrons are continually replenished by solar radiation, lightning, and heat from the Earth's core.

The science behind earthing lies in understanding these electrons and their interaction with the human body. Our bodies, being made up of atoms, are electrical in nature. Every heartbeat, nerve impulse, and cellular process involves the movement of electrons. It's a symphony of life conducted by nature's most fundamental particles.

When we make direct contact with the Earth, such as walking barefoot on the grass or sleeping on an earthing mat, we absorb these free electrons into our bodies. This absorption can neutralize the positively charged free radicals that are the byproducts of metabolic processes and are thought to cause inflammation and disease.

Several scientific studies support the theory. For instance, a study published in the Journal of Environmental and Public Health found that earthing changes the electrical activity in the brain, as shown by electroencephalograms. Meanwhile, other studies have shown that earthing can improve sleep, reduce pain, and decrease stress.

Earthing is also believed to influence the delicate balance of the autonomic nervous system, which controls our heart rate, digestion, respiratory rate, pupillary response, urination, and sexual arousal. This influence is because the Earth's electrons are a natural source of white noise, which can normalize biological rhythms, including circadian rhythm.

In essence, the science of earthing is a study of connections. It's about the connection between the Earth and our bodies, between the physical and the metaphysical, between the tangible world of atoms and the intangible world of energy. It's a reminder that we are not separate entities but an integral part of the universe's intricate web of life.

As we delve deeper into the science of earthing, we begin to see that it is not just a practice but a way of life, a holistic approach to well-being grounded in the universe's very fabric. It's a journey of discovery that begins with a single step, a barefoot step on the nurturing bosom of Mother Earth.

Earthing and Human Evolution

As we delve into the intricate dance between the Earth and human evolution, we must appreciate the profound relationship that has shaped our being. The human body evolved over millions of years, and our ancestors were intimately connected to the natural world for the vast majority of that time. This connection to the Earth was not simply a matter of proximity but a fundamental aspect of their existence.

As we transitioned over generations from a nomadic lifestyle to agricultural societies and eventually to today's urbanized and technologically advanced civilizations, our direct connection with the Earth's surface slowly faded. Shoes with insulating materials, such as rubber and plastic, became the norm, and lifestyles increasingly confined people indoors.

The concept of earthing suggests that many of the health challenges faced by contemporary society, such as chronic inflammation, increased stress levels, disrupted sleep patterns, and a weakened immune response, may, in part, be a consequence of this loss of electrical contact with the Earth. By reconnecting with the Earth's surface, earthing could restore a measure of the natural balance that the course of human evolution has disrupted.

Debunking Myths and Misconceptions about Earthing

In the realm of holistic health, earthing is a concept that has been both embraced and misunderstood. As we delve into the heart of this practice, it is essential to dispel some of the myths and misconceptions that have clouded its true essence.

One of the most prevalent misconceptions is that earthing is a new-age, pseudoscientific concept. This notion couldn't be further from the truth. Earthing, or grounding, is deeply rooted in the natural world and our ancestral connection. It is not a fleeting trend but a timeless practice that has been part of human life for millennia.

Another common myth is that earthing is merely about walking barefoot on the Earth. While this is a fundamental aspect of the practice, earthing encompasses much more. It is about fostering a deeper connection with the Earth's energy, which can be achieved through various methods, such as swimming in natural bodies of water, gardening, or even sleeping on earthing sheets.

A third misconception is that the benefits of earthing are purely psychological, a placebo effect. However, scientific studies have shown that earthing has tangible physiological effects. These include reduced inflammation, improved sleep, and enhanced wound healing. We will explore the need for further scientific research in later chapters.

Lastly, there is a myth that earthing is a cure-all solution. While earthing has numerous health benefits, it is not a panacea. It should be viewed as a complementary practice, part of a holistic approach to well-being that includes a balanced diet, regular exercise, and mental health care.

We will unpack these myths and misconceptions in a later chapter in a quest to shed light on the true nature of earthing. It is a practice rooted in our innate connection to the Earth, invites us to tap into the healing power of nature, and a practice that, combined with other healthful habits, can contribute to overall well-being.

As we move forward, let us embrace earthing for what it truly is - a natural, holistic approach to health as old as humanity itself.

Embracing Earthing as a Holistic Approach to Well-being

As we draw the curtain on this enlightening overview of earthing, it is essential to emphasize the holistic nature of this practice. Earthing, as we have discovered, is not merely a physical act of connecting with the Earth but a comprehensive approach to well-being that encompasses our existence's physical, emotional, and spiritual dimensions.

The Earth beneath our feet, often taken for granted, is a potent source of healing and rejuvenation. It is a silent, steadfast companion that has journeyed with us through the eons, bearing witness to our evolution, triumphs, and tribulations. By consciously reconnecting with this ancient ally through earthing, we are grounding ourselves physically and anchoring our lives in a broader, more profound context.

As we have seen, the practice of earthing is rooted in the wisdom of our ancestors, validated by modern science, and brought to life through practical techniques. It is a testament to the timeless truth that we are, in essence, children of the Earth, bound to it by the laws of nature and the rhythms of life. By embracing earthing, we acknowledge this profound connection and harness its power for our well-being.

The health benefits of earthing, ranging from improved sleep and reduced inflammation to enhanced immunity and emotional stability, are impressive. However, the true value of earthing lies not merely in these tangible outcomes, but in the subtle, transformative shifts it can bring about in our perception and experience of life. By grounding ourselves in the Earth, we are grounding ourselves in the present moment, in the here and now, which is the wellspring of holistic health and happiness.

In a world riddled with myths and misconceptions about health and well-being, earthing is a simple, natural, and accessible practice that anyone can incorporate into their lives. It is a gentle reminder that we are not separate from nature but an integral part of it and that our well-being is inextricably linked to the health of the Earth.

In conclusion, embracing earthing as a holistic approach to well-being is not just about adopting a new practice but about reclaiming ancient wisdom, rekindling a forgotten relationship, and redefining our place in the grand scheme of things. It is about coming home to ourselves, the Earth, and the interconnected web of life that sustains us all.

Chapter Summary

- Earthing, or grounding, is the practice of connecting directly with the Earth's natural electric charge, a concept deeply rooted in many different cultures and traditions. However, modern lifestyles have led to a disconnect from this fundamental connection, impacting our health and well-being.

- The historical roots of earthing trace back to our ancestors who lived in close communion with nature. Indigenous cultures revered the Earth as a source of life and healing; even scientific studies explored the effects of grounding.
- The science behind earthing lies in understanding the Earth's negatively charged free electrons and their interaction with the human body. Direct contact with the Earth allows these electrons to flow into our bodies, neutralizing positively charged free radicals that cause inflammation and disease.
- The advent of industrialisation and urbanization and resulting disconnection from the Earth's electrical rhythms has coincided with the rise of many of the health challenges faced by contemporary society. Reconnecting with the Earth through earthing could potentially restore the natural balance that has been disrupted by the course of human evolution.
- Common misconceptions about earthing include it being a new-age concept, only about walking barefoot, its purely psychological benefits, and it being a cure-all solution. However, earthing is a timeless practice with tangible physiological effects and should be considered part of a holistic approach to well-being.
- Embracing earthing as a holistic approach to well-being is about acknowledging our profound connection with the Earth and harnessing its power for our health.
- Earthing is a simple, natural, and accessible practice anyone can incorporate into their lives. It's about reclaiming a pearl of ancient wisdom, rekindling a forgotten relationship with the Earth, and redefining our place in the interconnected web of life.

2

EARTHING THROUGH THE AGES

I mmersed in the tapestry of history, the concept of earthing and grounding emerges not as a transient trend but as a venerable tradition, rich with the echoes of ancient wisdom. Long before the term "earthing" was coined, our ancestors engaged in grounding practices, intuitively seeking the Earth's nurturing touch as a source of healing and vitality.

The ancients lived in a world where their daily lives were intertwined with the rhythms of the Earth. Their bare feet kissed the soil, they slept under the stars, and toiled with the elements in a harmonious dance of survival and spirituality. This intrinsic connection to the Earth was not incidental to their existence but a fundamental thread woven into the very fabric of their cultural and spiritual practices.

In civilizations such as those of ancient Mesopotamia, Egypt, and India, grounding was an integral part of life. The Mesopotamians revered the Earth as a bountiful giver of life. They engaged in rituals that involved direct contact with the soil, celebrating the cycles of growth and harvest. In Egypt, the connection to the Earth was embodied in their reverence for the Nile's life-giving floods and the fertile mud synonymous with regeneration and rebirth.

Across the seas, the practice of grounding in ancient India had spiritual significance. The Vedic texts, some of the oldest sacred scriptures in the world, speak of the Earth as a divine mother, "Bhumi," whose body is to be honored and cared for. Yogis and ascetics would meditate and practice yoga on the bare ground, seeking enlightenment and a profound connection with the Earth's boundless energy.

In ancient China, the notion of "Qi," or life force, was pivotal to their understanding of health and the universe. Traditional Chinese medicine emphasizes the balance of this vital energy, and grounding practices such as walking barefoot were believed to help harmonize the body's Qi with that of the Earth.

Even Greek philosophers like Aristotle and Hippocrates acknowledged the importance of the elements, including the Earth, to maintain balance and health. They championed natural therapies, including using earthen materials in medicine and walking barefoot to absorb the Earth's energies.

These ancient rituals of grounding were not only about physical health but also about maintaining a spiritual and emotional balance. The Earth was revered as a living entity, a mother who provided and sustained life. By forging a close physical connection with the ground, our ancestors believed they could tap into this life force, enhancing their well-being and aligning themselves with the natural order of the cosmos.

As we pivot to examining earthing in indigenous cultures, it is essential to appreciate that while grounding practices may vary across different societies and periods, the underlying principle remains the same: the Earth is a source of healing, stability, and connection that transcends cultural boundaries. The wisdom of our ancestors serves as a testament to the enduring power of this simple yet profound act of touching the Earth with our bare skin.

Earthing in Indigenous Cultures

Throughout the tapestry of human history, the practice of earthing has woven itself into the fabric of numerous indigenous cultures around the world. These communities have long recognized the Earth as a source of healing and sustenance, not merely a physical terrain but a living entity that offers energy to all life forms.

In the lush embrace of the Amazonian rainforests, indigenous tribes have practiced walking barefoot as a way to absorb the Earth's vital energy. They believe that the soles of the feet are channels for the spirit of the Earth to enter the body and harmonize with their own life force.

Similarly, the Aboriginal peoples of Australia, with their deep spiritual connection to the land, have a concept known as "Dadirri," which translates to a profound, spiritual act of listening and quiet, still awareness. This practice involves sitting on the ground and connecting with the Earth's rhythms, a form of grounding that fosters a profound sense of peace and interconnectedness with nature.

In North America, many Native American traditions emphasize the importance of walking barefoot on the Earth to connect with the "Great Spirit." Ceremonies such as the Sundance, where flesh meets soil, are considered sacred and imbued with life-giving properties. Participants seek healing and wisdom through this intimate Earthly bond.

The Maasai of East Africa, renowned for their harmonious coexistence with nature, have long valued grounding as they stood barefoot on the Earth. They trust in the Earth's energy, absorbed through the feet, to restore physical strength and endurance, qualities essential to their nomadic lifestyle and survival.

Venturing to the Pacific, the indigenous Hawaiians have a concept called "Aloha 'Āina," a deep love of the land. They see the land as an ancestor, a family member to be cared for and respected. They tread barefoot, anchoring themselves to lava rocks and sandy shores, to engage in a reciprocal exchange of mana, or spiritual energy, nurturing both the land and its inhabitants.

These practices, deeply rooted in the spiritual and cultural fabric of indigenous communities, affirm a universal truth: the Earth is a source of life, not just in the biological sense but as a wellspring of spiritual energy. Grounding bridges the physical and the metaphysical, a means humans have sought to align themselves with the natural world's rhythms and cycles.

As we transition to the modern world, it becomes clear that the whirlwind of technological progress and urban sprawl has cast a shadow over the wisdom of these indigenous practices. The disconnection from the Earth's natural energy is a touching reflection of the wider disengagement from nature itself, a disconnect that influences our collective health and well-being. With this in mind, we can begin to understand the profound importance of reconnecting with the Earth, as our ancestors once did, to reclaim a sense of balance and harmony in our everyday lives.

The Lost Connection in Modern Times

As we trace the footprints of our ancestors, we find a stark contrast in our modern lives. Our once profound connection with the Earth has become a faint echo in the cacophony of contemporary society. This disconnection is not merely symbolic but a literal separation from the electrical embrace of our planet.

In bygone eras, our predecessors walked barefoot upon the soil, slept on the ground, and cultivated the land with their hands. They existed in a perpetual embrace with the Earth's natural electrical currents, an interaction that was as much a part of life as the air they breathed.

Fast forward to the present, and our communication with the Earth has undergone a momentous shift. Modern footwear, with its insulating rubber and plastic soles, has elevated us millimeters from the Earth's surface, yet miles away from its electrical touch. Our homes, too, have become insulated islands, with floors of wood, carpet, and tile that disturb the conductive thread linking us to the ground.

The urbanization of our environments has amplified this effect. Cities, with their asphalt jungles and concrete canopies, stifle the natural flow of electrons between the Earth and our bodies. The rise of electronic devices and the presence of electromagnetic fields have created an invisible smog that further obscures our primal connection to the planet.

Our lifestyles have drifted to favor convenience and efficiency, often at the expense of our connection with nature. We spend most of our days indoors, under artificial lighting, surrounded by walls that shield us from the elemental embrace of the Earth. The simple act of walking barefoot outside has become an oddity, a relic of a bygone era viewed through nostalgia or the pursuit of leisure.

The consequences of this lost connection are not just philosophical. Emerging research hints that the lack of direct contact with the Earth's surface may have material health implications. In this context, the modern disconnection from the Earth symbolizes not just our detachment from nature but a literal gap in our physiological functioning. The insulating materials that define our modern existence—rubber, plastic, synthetic fibers—act as barriers to the Earth's natural healing potential.

At this juncture of tradition and technology, we must contemplate the impact of our choices on our health and well-being. The following section will explore the resurgence of interest in earthing as many people seek to rekindle this ancient practice and reintegrate the Earth's energy into their lives. The revival of earthing in the 21st century is not merely a trend but a collective yearning to reconnect with the source of our existence, a beckoning to rediscover the grounding force that has sustained humanity through the ages.

Revival of Earthing in the 21st Century

In the 21st century, a profound shift began to stir in the collective consciousness of humanity. The relentless pace of modern life began to take its toll, and a yearning for reconnection with nature's simplicity and healing rhythms began to emerge. Amidst this backdrop, the practice of earthing found new life, a revival that beckoned the weary back to the nurturing embrace of the Earth's electric heart.

This resurgence was not a sudden spark but a slow, steady flame that grew brighter as the years progressed. It was kindled by a confluence of factors: a burgeoning awareness of alternative health practices, a growing body of scientific research on the benefits of earthing, and the stories of those who had experienced profound transformations in their health and well-being.

The revival was marked by a rediscovery of the intrinsic connection between the Earth's surface and the human body. Trailblazers in earthing science began to unravel the mysteries of this connection, exploring how the Earth's natural electric charge could influence the body's physiological processes. They argued that the modern lifestyle had disturbed the electrical contact between humans and the Earth, potentially giving rise to a host of inflammation-driven ailments.

As the evidence mounted, a fresh narrative began to crystallize. The Earth emerged not as a mere stage for human endeavors but as a dynamic contributor to our vitality and well-being. Its surface, thrumming with a subtle yet potent energy, appeared to have a stabilizing effect on the body's bioelectrical landscape.

The revival of earthing in the 21st century was also a story of innovation. Visionaries and entrepreneurs saw the potential to reconnect people with the Earth's energy, even in the most urban environments. They crafted a range of new earthing products, from conductive mats and sheets to grounding footwear, allowing people to tap into the Earth's energy indoors or on the go. These products were designed to bridge the gap between the modern lifestyle and the ancient practice of earthing, making the benefits more accessible to a population largely estranged from the natural world.

The revival of earthing in the 21st century was not merely a return to an ancient practice but an evolution. It signified a merging of ancestral wisdom with modern science, acknowledging that we must not lose touch with the elemental forces that sustain us in our pursuit of advancement. As we continue navigating the complexities of contemporary life, earthing stands as a testament to the enduring human desire for connection—not just with each other but with the very ground beneath our feet.

Earthing Movements and Communities

As we delve deeper into the historical tapestry of earthing, we find that the resurgence of interest in the 21st century has given rise to various movements and communities advocating for the practice. Though diverse in their approaches, these groups are bound by a collective appreciation for the Earth's grounding energy and have been instrumental in the revival of earthing.

A counter-movement emerged in the wake of the digital revolution, calling for a return to nature and simplicity. This movement, often called the 'Earthing Movement,' emphasizes reconnecting with the Earth's natural electrical charge. It responds to the growing scientific research suggesting that such a connection can yield significant health benefits, including reduced inflammation, improved sleep, and general well-being.

The Earthing Movement is not a monolith but a mosaic of individuals and groups, weaving their thread into the larger narrative. Among these are health and wellness practitioners who incorporate earthing into their holistic health regimes. Naturopaths, chiropractors, and massage therapists often recommend earthing with their treatments.

Another vibrant strand within the earthing tapestry is the network of online communities. These digital spaces are repositories of shared knowledge and support systems for those new to the practice. They are hubs for exchanging tips on the best earthing techniques and the most effective equipment, from grounding mats to conductive footwear.

Earthing retreats and workshops have emerged around the globe, offering immersive experiences in serene natural settings. These sanctuaries often combine earthing with other wellness practices, such as yoga, meditation, and mindful walking, to create holistic wellness packages. Participants leave grounded in the literal sense and with a deeper understanding of how to integrate earthing into their daily lives.

The Earthing Movement has also witnessed the rise of advocates and influencers who have taken to various media platforms to spread the word. Books, documentaries, and podcasts have played a significant role in popularizing the concept. These resources often feature personal testimonies, interviews with experts, and discussions on the latest research, helping to demystify earthing for the general public.

At the heart of these movements and communities lies a profound respect for the Earth and an acknowledgment of our intrinsic bond with it. This collective awareness has spurred a cultural shift that recognizes the importance of our environment not just for its resources but for its healing potential.

As these earthing communities expand, they stand at the threshold of a new epoch where the interplay of technology and nature seeks harmony. They are not merely passive participants in this age-old practice but active pioneers of a philosophy that could shape the future of human health and well-being. With feet planted firmly on the ground, these communities look forward to a future where the Earth's energy is not taken for granted but is harnessed as a vital component of living a balanced and healthy life.

Chapter Summary

- Earthing has deep historical significance, with roots stretching back to ancient traditions and our ancestors' intuitive understanding of the Earth's healing properties.
- Ancient civilizations, including Mesopotamia, Egypt, India, China, and Greece, recognized the importance of grounding in their daily lives and spiritual practices.
- Indigenous cultures worldwide have maintained a deep connection with the Earth, viewing it as a spiritual energy and well-being source.
- The modern era has seen a disconnection from the Earth due to urbanization, insulated living, and the prevalence of synthetic materials, leading to potential health implications.
- A revival of earthing in the 21st century is driven by a growing body of scientific research and a desire to reconnect with nature for improved health and vitality.
- The resurgence of earthing has led to new products and innovations that facilitate grounding in urban environments.
- The Earthing Movement comprises health practitioners, online communities, retreats, and media influencers promoting the practice and its benefits.
- Earthing communities are growing, advocating for a balanced integration of technology and nature to harness the Earth's energy for a healthier life.

3

THE SCIENCE BEHIND EARTHING

I n the heart of our existence, we are intimately entwined with the natural world. The air we breathe, the water we drink, and the food we eat are all gifts from Mother Earth. Yet, we often forget this primal connection in our modern, technologically driven lives. Earthing invites us to rekindle this bond, to ground ourselves in the nurturing embrace of our planet.

The human body moves to an electrical rhythm that is as essential as it is invisible. Our hearts beat thanks to electrical signals, our nervous system communicates through electrical impulses, and even our cells engage in electrical activities fundamental to their function. Within this context, we explore the relationship between electrical fields and the human body, a relationship at the heart of the practice of earthing.

Connecting directly with the Earth's surface allows us to tap into the Earth's natural, subtle electric charge. Due to countless factors, including solar and cosmic radiation and lightning hitting the Earth's surface, this charge creates a vast reservoir of negatively charged free electrons. When we make direct contact with the Earth, these electrons flow into our bodies, which has profound implications for our health and well-being.

The concept of earthing may seem simple, even primitive. Yet, it is anything but. It is a complex, fascinating interplay of physics, biology, ecology, a dance of electrons and cells, energy and matter. It is a testament to the intricate, delicate balance of life, a balance that we, as part of the web of life, are intrinsically a part of.

This chapter will delve into the science behind earthing, unraveling its mysteries and exploring its implications for human health. We will journey from the vast expanse of the cosmos to the microscopic world of our cells, from the ancient wisdom of our ancestors to the cutting-edge research of modern science.

As we embark on this journey, let us remember that earthing is not just a scientific concept or a health practice. It is a way of life, a holistic approach to well-being that invites us to reconnect with our roots, reclaim our place in the natural world, and rediscover the healing power of Mother Earth.

The Physics of Earthing: Understanding Earth's Electromagnetic Field

In the heart of our planet, a ceaseless dance of molten iron generates a powerful electromagnetic field that envelops the Earth. This invisible yet potent force, known as the Earth's electromagnetic field, is a fundamental aspect of our planet's identity and a key player in the intriguing concept of earthing.

To comprehend the physics of earthing, we must first delve into the nature of this field. The Earth's electromagnetic field is a dynamic entity, pulsating with the rhythm of the planet's core. It extends thousands of kilometers into space, forming a protective shield against harmful solar radiation. This field is not merely a planetary defense mechanism but also a source of natural, subtle energy that permeates every inch of the Earth's surface.

Earthing, or grounding, connects our bodies to this omnipresent energy. It is as simple as walking barefoot on the grass, swimming in the sea, or touching a tree. Engaging in these activities forms a direct, physical link with the Earth's electromagnetic field. This connection allows the transfer of electrons from the Earth to our bodies, a process believed to have profound implications for our health and well-being.

The Earth's surface carries a negative electrical charge due to count-less lightning strikes occurring worldwide every day. When we ground ourselves, we absorb these negative ions into our bodies. This absorption can neutralize the positive ions, or free radicals, often associated with inflammation and disease.

The physics of earthing is a fascinating blend of geophysics, biology, and chemistry. It is a testament to the interconnectedness of all things, a reminder that we are not separate entities but integral parts of a vast, complex system. It is a call to return to our roots, reconnect with the Earth, and harness its electromagnetic field's healing power.

In the following sections, we will explore the biological implications of earthing and delve into the confluence of ancient wisdom and modern science. As we journey through these topics, I invite you to keep an open mind, question, explore, and, most importantly, connect with the Earth beneath your feet.

Biological Implications: How Earthing Influences Human Health

In the heart of nature, where the earth's pulse beats in rhythm with our own, we find a profound connection that transcends the physical. This section delves into the biological implications of earthing, exploring how this ancient practice influences human health in subtle and significant ways.

The human body, a marvel of biological engineering, is an intricate network of systems and processes working in harmony. It is a living, breathing entity constantly interacting with its environment. And the earth, with its vast electromagnetic field, is a significant part of this envi-ronment. When we engage in earthing, we immerse ourselves in this field, allowing our bodies to absorb the earth's natural, healing energy.

Our bodies are composed of many cells, each with its complex system of molecules. These molecules engage in various chemical reactions, many of which involve the exchange of electrons. Electrons are the currency of chemical reactions, facilitating the bonds between atoms and playing a pivotal role in energy production within our cells.

This transfer of electrons is made possible by the skin, our body's largest organ, which acts as a conductor, allowing us to interface with the Earth's surface. When our skin comes into contact with the ground, the Earth's electrons are believed to be absorbed into the body. These electrons have the potential to neutralize positively charged free radicals, which are known to contribute to inflammation and oxidative stress. By providing a steady stream of electrons, the Earth may act as a natural antioxidant, helping to reduce the chronic inflammation often at the root of many health disorders.

Earthing and Inflammation

At the core of earthing's biological impact is the concept of inflammation. Inflammation, in its simplest form, is a vital part of our body's defense mechanism. However, chronic inflammation can lead to a range of health issues, from heart disease to autoimmune disorders. Earthing has been shown to reduce inflammation by neutralizing excess positive ions in the body through the influx of negative ions from the Earth, which act as natural antioxidants, combating inflammation at a cellular level.

Scientific studies have begun to shed light on the fascinating relationship between earthing and inflammation. Research utilizing thermal imaging has demonstrated that after grounding, the redness and heat associated with inflammation are reduced, indicating a reduced inflammatory response.

The implications of these findings are profound. By helping reduce chronic inflammation, earthing could aid in the prevention and management of various inflammatory diseases. It is a simple yet powerful finding that harnesses the Earth's potential to promote healing and restore balance within the body.

It is important to note, however, that while the initial research is promising, the field of earthing science is still in its infancy. The mechanisms by which grounding influences inflammation are not fully understood, and more rigorous, controlled studies are needed to substantiate these early findings and to unravel the therapeutic potential of earthing.

Impact on Circadian Rhythms and the Nervous System

In the intricate dance of life, our bodies are attuned to the earth's natural rhythms. One of the most fundamental of these processes is the circadian rhythm, the internal clock that orchestrates our sleep-wake cycle, hormones, and eating habits, among other bodily functions. By aligning ourselves with the earth's natural rhythms, we can promote better sleep, enhance mood, and improve overall well-being.

Research suggests that earthing and grounding can influence circadian rhythms by aligning the body's internal clock with the Earth's natural electromagnetic signals. These signals are believed to act as a universal synchronizing pulse for life on our planet. Our connection to these natural rhythms has been disrupted in a modern world where exposure to artificial light and electronic devices is widespread.

By re-establishing our connection with the Earth, earthing may help recalibrate our internal clocks. The grounding effect is posited to normalize the daily cortisol rhythm, promoting better sleep, more consistent energy levels throughout the day, and a general sense of alertness and well-being.

The influence of earthing extends to the nervous system as well. The Earth's electromagnetic field can help balance the autonomic nervous system, promoting relaxation and reducing stress. This calming effect can have profound implications for mental health, offering a natural, holistic approach to managing anxiety and depression.

Earthing's impact on human health is a testament to the interconnectedness of all life. It reminds us that we are not separate entities but part of a larger world. We tap into the earth's healing energy by grounding ourselves, fostering balance and harmony within our bodies and minds.

Unveiling the Mysteries of Earthing

As we draw this chapter to a close, it is essential to reflect on our embarked journey, exploring the intriguing science behind earthing. We have delved into the physics of our planet's electromagnetic field, the biological implications of earthing on human health, and the confluence of ancient wisdom and contemporary research.

As we have discovered, earthing is not merely a practice but a way of life, a philosophy that encourages us to reconnect with the natural world. It is a call to step away from our technologically saturated lives and ground ourselves, literally and metaphorically, in the earth beneath our feet.

The science behind earthing is compelling, suggesting that touching the earth can profoundly affect our health and well-being. It can help reduce inflammation, improve sleep, increase energy, and enhance our overall wellness. But beyond the scientific, earthing offers a deeper, more spiritual connection to the world. It reminds us that we are not separate entities but part of a vast, interconnected web of life.

Earthing provides a pathway to wholeness in a world that often feels fragmented and disconnected. It invites us to slow down, to feel the earth beneath our feet, to listen to the rhythm of nature, and to remember our place within it. It is a practice accessible to all, regardless of age, health, or location. All it requires is a willingness to step outside, feel the earth beneath our feet, and open ourselves to nature's healing power.

Earthing is more than just a scientific concept; it is a call to return to our roots, reconnect with the earth, and embrace a more grounded, holistic approach to well-being. It is a journey of discovery, a path to wellness, and a reminder of our inherent connection to the natural world. As we step forward, let us do so with our feet firmly planted on the ground, our hearts open to the wisdom of the earth, and our minds attuned to the science that unveils the mysteries of earthing.

Chapter Summary

- Earthing allows us to tap into the Earth's natural, subtle electric charge. This connection can be achieved through various means, such as walking barefoot on grass, lying on the beach, or using conductive systems indoors.

- The Earth's electromagnetic field is a source of natural, subtle energy that permeates every inch of the Earth's surface. When we ground ourselves, we absorb these negative ions into our bodies, which can neutralize the positive ions, or free radicals, often associated with inflammation and disease.

- Earthing has profound biological implications, including reducing inflammation, influencing our circadian rhythms, and balancing the autonomic nervous system. These effects can lead to improved sleep, enhanced mood, reduced stress, and overall better well-being.

- Modern science is exploring the ancient practice of earthing, finding that the flow of electrons from the Earth to our bodies can neutralize free radicals, alleviate inflammation, improve sleep, increase energy, and enhance overall well-being. It also suggests that earthing can help reduce stress and anxiety, improve mood, and promote a sense of calm and tranquility.

- Earthing is not just a practice but a way of life, a philosophy that encourages us to reconnect with the natural world. It offers a deeper, more spiritual connection to the world around us, reminding us that we are part of a vast, interconnected web of life.

- Embracing earthing as a holistic approach to well-being involves understanding its scientific basis, appreciating its roots in ancient wisdom, and integrating it into our daily lives. It is a journey of discovery, a path to wellness, and a reminder of our inherent connection to the natural world.

4

EARTHING AND HEALTH: THE HEALING POWER OF THE EARTH

I n the grand tapestry of life, we humans are threads woven intricately into the fabric of nature. We are not separate from the Earth, but rather, we are an integral part of it. This fundamental truth, often overlooked in the hustle and bustle of modern life, forms the basis of earthing. Earthing is about re-establishing our connection with the Earth and harnessing its healing power.

This chapter will delve into the many benefits of earthing for physical and mental health. As we embark on this journey, let us remember that earthing is not just a practice but a way of life. It is a holistic approach to health and well-being that recognizes the interconnectedness of all things. It is a reminder that we are not separate from the Earth but are a part of it. And by reconnecting with the Earth, we are, in essence, reconnecting with ourselves and finding our place in the grand tapestry of life.

Earthing and Physical Health: A Deep Dive into the Benefits

The earth beneath our feet, often taken for granted, holds a profound secret. It is a source of healing, a reservoir of energy, and a conduit for transferring life-sustaining elements. This section delves into the physical health benefits of earthing, exploring what happens to our body when we make direct contact with the earth's surface.

In its intricate design, the human body is a bioelectrical organism living in an electrical world. Our heart, brain, and nervous system are all electrical sub-systems operating within this larger system. The earth, too, is an electrical entity, pulsating with natural, subtle frequencies. Earthing, or grounding, reconnects our bodies to this natural electrical state, creating a conduit for the earth's healing energy.

One of the most significant benefits of earthing is its potential to reduce inflammation, as we explored in earlier chapters. Inflammation, often the body's response to injury, can become chronic and contribute to various health issues like heart disease, arthritis, and even cancer. The earth's surface is teeming with negatively charged electrons, and when we make direct contact with it, these electrons are absorbed into our bodies. These electrons neutralize positively charged free radicals that cause inflammation, effectively reducing it and promoting healing.

This simple act is believed to offer a natural, profound remedy for pain reduction and recovery enhancement. This is because the electrons help restore the body's natural electrical state, often disrupted by injury or illness. Preliminary studies have also shown that grounding can influence physiological processes, such as improving blood flow and viscosity, which are essential for healing and recovery.

As we also explored earlier, earthing can help improve sleep and regulate the body's circadian rhythms. The earth's magnetic field influences these rhythms, and direct contact with the earth can help synchronize our internal biological clocks with the earth's natural cycles. This synchronization can improve sleep, increase energy, and overall better health.

Finally, earthing can improve cardiovascular health. Studies have shown that grounding can normalize blood pressure and blood flow, reducing the risk of cardiovascular disease. This is likely due to the calming effect earthing has on the nervous system and the body's physiological processes. In addition, the anti-inflammatory effects of earthing can prevent cardiovascular diseases caused by chronic inflammation. By mitigating stress and its physiological repercussions, earthing may help maintain a healthier blood pressure profile.

In essence, earthing is a natural, holistic approach to health that harnesses the earth's healing power. It is a testament to the interconnectedness of all life and a reminder of our inherent bond with nature. As we delve deeper into the benefits of earthing, we begin to see the earth not just as our home but as a source of vitality, wellness, and healing.

Earthing and Mental Well-being: The Earth's Role in Emotional Balance

In the heart of our modern, fast-paced world, where technology and artificial environments dominate, we often find ourselves disconnected from the natural world. This disconnection, some argue, has not only physical but also profound psychological implications. This section delves into the intriguing relationship between earthing and mental well-being, exploring how reconnecting with the Earth can help restore emotional balance and promote mental health.

In its infinite wisdom and timeless rhythm, the Earth has always been a source of solace and healing. It is a sanctuary where we can retreat, recharge, and realign. From a biological perspective, earthing influences the intricate dynamics of our body's electrical system. The Earth's surface is brimming with negatively charged ions, which, when absorbed into our bodies, can help neutralize harmful free radicals and reduce inflammation. This process benefits not only our physical health but also our mental state. Inflammation has been linked to various mental health disorders, including depression and anxiety. Earthing can help alleviate these conditions and promote emotional balance by reducing inflammation.

Earthing can help regulate our body's circadian rhythms and sleep quality, which are closely tied to stress and anxiety. Disruptions in this cycle can lead to sleep disorders, mood swings, and cognitive impairment. We can help reset our biological clock, improve sleep quality, and enhance mood and cognitive function by grounding ourselves to the Earth.

Beyond the biological benefits, earthing also offers a psychological reprieve. It allows us to step away from the chaos of modern life and immerse ourselves in the calming embrace of nature. This immersion can help reduce stress, clear the mind, and foster a sense of peace and tranquility. It is a form of mindfulness, a way to be present in the moment and reconnect with our roots. Anecdotal evidence and preliminary studies have shown that those who practice earthing report a reduction in their stress levels and an improvement in their overall emotional well-being. They describe feeling more centered, less reactive to stressors, and more at peace.

Moreover, earthing has been shown to influence our autonomic nervous system, which controls many of our body's unconscious functions, including heart rate, digestion, and, crucially, our stress response. Studies have shown that earthing can shift our autonomic nervous system towards parasympathetic dominance, often called the 'rest and digest' state. This state is associated with feelings of calm and relaxation, a stark contrast to the 'fight or flight' response of sympathetic dominance often triggered by our modern, stressful lifestyles.

In essence, earthing is not merely a physical act but a holistic practice that nurtures our mental well-being. It is a gentle reminder of our inherent connection to the Earth, a connection that can heal, balance, and rejuvenate. As we move forward in this chapter, we will explore practical ways to incorporate earthing into our daily lives and delve into real-life experiences of its healing power.

Reconnecting with Earth, Reconnecting with Self

As we draw this exploration of earthing to a close, we find ourselves standing at the precipice of a new understanding, a new connection to the world beneath our feet. We have journeyed through the science and explored the physical and mental health benefits of earthing. Now, we stand ready to embrace the earth's energy in our lives and reconnect with the ground beneath us for a healthier future.

The journey we've embarked upon, from understanding the intricate workings of the human mind to the transformative power of earthing, has led us to a simple yet profound truth: reconnecting with the Earth is, in essence, reconnecting with ourselves.

In all its raw, unadulterated beauty, the Earth is not just a physical entity we inhabit. It is a living, breathing organism that we are intrinsically linked to, a symbiotic relationship that has been forgotten in our modern, technology-driven world. But as we've discovered, this connection is not merely physical. It is deeply psychological and spiritual, influencing our mental well-being in ways we are only beginning to understand.

Earthing, as we've learned, is not a complex practice reserved for the enlightened or the adventurous. It is a natural pathway to mental equilibrium, a simple act of stepping barefoot on the Earth, feeling the cool grass or the warm sand beneath our feet, and allowing the Earth's natural energy to ground us, balance us, and heal us.

Earthing is not just a practice. It's a way of life, a way of being, a way of reconnecting with the Earth, and, in doing so, reconnecting with ourselves. It's about understanding that we are not separate from the Earth, but a part of it, a part of its energy, its rhythm, its life. In this understanding, we find not just mental well-being but a sense of belonging, a sense of home, and a sense of self.

In its infinite wisdom and enduring patience, the Earth has always been there, waiting for us to remember our connection to it. It has been waiting for us to take off our shoes, feel the cool grass or the warm sand beneath our feet, and remember that we are not separate from the world but intrinsically part of it.

In reconnecting with the Earth, we are not just healing ourselves but also healing our world. We acknowledge our place in the natural order and responsibility to care for the earth as it cares for us.

As we stand on the brink of a healthier future, remember that the earth is our ally, healer, and home. Remember to walk gently, tread lightly, and honor the sacred ground beneath our feet. In doing so, we honor ourselves, our health, and the health of generations to come.

In conclusion, earthing is a practice and a way of life. It is a path to health, well-being, and a deeper understanding of our place in the world. It is a journey that begins with a single step and a moment of connection.

And it is a journey that, once begun, can transform our lives in ways we never imagined. So, let us step forward, reconnect, and embrace the earth's healing power. In doing so, we embrace a healthier, more holistic future.

Chapter Summary

- Earthing is believed to have numerous health benefits due to the Earth's natural healing power.
- Research has suggested that earthing can reduce inflammation, improve sleep and regulate the body's circadian rhythms, enhance the body's natural healing processes, and improve cardiovascular health. These benefits are attributed to the neutralization of free radicals, and the calming effect earthing has on the nervous system.
- Beyond physical health, earthing also has significant benefits for mental well-being. It can help reduce stress, clear the mind, foster a sense of peace and tranquility, and promote emotional balance. It also helps regulate our body's circadian rhythms, improving sleep quality and enhancing mood and cognitive function.
- Earthing serves as a natural pathway to mental equilibrium. By connecting with the earth, we can tap into its natural equilibrium, grounding our thoughts, quieting our emotions, and fostering a sense of inner peace.
- Earthing is not just about reconnecting with the earth but also about reconnecting with oneself. It's about grounding the mind in the present, in the tangible reality of the earth beneath our feet, leading to greater mental well-being.
- Earthing is not a new-age fad or a fleeting trend but a return to our roots and a reconnection with the natural world. It is a recognition of the earth as a source of healing and well-being that we have too often overlooked in our modern, fast-paced lives.

- Earthing is not just a practice but a way of life. It is a path to health, well-being, and a deeper understanding of our place in the world. It is a journey that begins with a single step and moment of connection and can transform our lives in ways we never imagined.

5

THE ART OF GROUNDING: PRACTICAL TECHNIQUES TO INCORPORATE INTO YOUR DAILY ROUTINE

Though seemingly independent, our existence is deeply interconnected with the world around us. We are but threads woven intricately into the fabric of the universe. This interconnectedness extends beyond our relationships with other beings to our relationship with Earth. The Earth, our home, is not just a passive stage on which the drama of life unfolds but an active participant in our lives, offering us its energy, vitality, and healing power. This chapter invites you to embrace this energy through the practice of earthing.

As we navigate an increasingly disconnected and digital world, earthing and grounding offers a path back to our roots, a way to re-establish our bond with the Earth and tap into its restorative power.

The Earth's energy is not a mystical or elusive force. It is tangible, measurable, and accessible to all. It pulses beneath our feet, courses through the air we breathe, and permeates the world around us. When we ground ourselves, we align our body's energy with that of the Earth, creating a natural balance that promotes health, wellness, and harmony.

Embracing the Earth's energy is not merely about physical contact with the ground. It is about cultivating a conscious awareness of our connection with the Earth, acknowledging its presence in our lives, and honoring its role in our well-being. It is about grounding our thoughts, emotions, and spirit as much as our physical body.

As we delve deeper into this chapter, we will explore practical techniques for daily grounding and provide guidance on different ways you can incorporate earthing into your daily life.

As you journey through these pages, may you find inspiration to embrace the Earth's energy, to ground yourself in its rhythm, and to weave this practice into the fabric of your life. For in grounding, we not only connect with the Earth, but we also connect with ourselves, with our essence, and with the universal energy that binds us all.

Barefoot Earthing

Barefoot earthing is one of the simplest and most profound methods to reconnect with the Earth's natural electric charge. This practice involves making direct contact with the Earth's surface by walking, standing, or sitting barefoot on natural grounds such as soil, grass, sand, or even concrete, provided it is not sealed or painted.

The human body is composed of many electrical circuits, and the Earth itself is an electrical planet pulsating with a subtle yet constant electromagnetic field. The soles of our feet contain a rich network of nerves and acupuncture points, and when they make direct contact with the Earth, they allow us to absorb the Earth's electrons. These electrons are nature's anti-inflammatories, and they help to balance the body's charge, reduce inflammation, and promote physiological and electrical stability.

Barefoot earthing is not a novel or new concept. Our ancestors walked the Earth without the barrier of non-conductive materials such as rubber or plastic in modern footwear. Doing so made them naturally grounded for most of their waking hours. Today, we have largely lost this constant physical connection due to the insulating nature of our shoes and high-rise living structures.

To practice barefoot earthing, find a natural space where you feel safe and comfortable. This could be your backyard, a local park, a beach, or a forest path. Begin by simply standing still, feeling the texture and temperature of the Earth beneath your feet. Take deep breaths and allow your-self to become present in the moment. Gradually, you can start to walk gently, paying attention to the sensation of each step as your feet make contact with the ground.

As you engage in this practice, being mindful of your environment is essential. Ensure the area is free from hazards such as sharp objects, harmful organisms, or toxic substances. In an urban setting, a patch of grass or a stretch of concrete that has direct contact with the Earth can also serve as a grounding surface.

For those new to barefoot earthing, it's advisable to start with short sessions and gradually increase the duration as your body acclimates to the sensation and the practice. Some individuals may experience a tingling sensation or warmth in their feet as they ground themselves, which is a normal response as the body begins to absorb the Earth's elec-trons. Those who regularly practice barefoot earthing often report a sense of calmness, reduced stress levels, and an overall improvement in well-being.

Incorporating barefoot earthing into your daily routine can be as simple as taking a few moments each day to step outside and connect with the Earth. Whether it's during a morning ritual, a break in your workday, or a leisurely walk in the evening, grounding can be a powerful tool for re-establishing our connection with the natural world and enhancing our health and vitality.

As we explore the various ways to ground ourselves, it's important to remember that barefoot earthing is just one of many techniques. For those who may not have regular access to natural surfaces or for whom outdoor grounding is not practical, there are alternative methods and equipment designed to simulate the effects of earthing, which we will delve into in the following section.

Earthing Equipment

As we transition from the tactile pleasures of barefoot earthing, where our skin directly contacts the Earth's surface, we now delve into the realm of earthing equipment. This technology is designed to provide the benefits of earthing without the need to be outdoors or in direct contact with the ground. It's particularly useful for those living in urban environments or when going barefoot outside isn't practical or possible.

Earthing equipment comes in various forms, each designed to cater to different lifestyles and preferences. Let's explore some of the most common types and how to use them effectively.

- **Earthing mats:** These are the most versatile pieces of earthing equipment. Typically made from a conductive material, such as carbon or silver mesh, these mats can be placed under your feet while working at a desk, under your keyboard and mouse, or even in bed while you sleep. To use an earthing mat, plug it into a grounded electrical outlet or connect it to a grounding rod placed directly in the Earth outside. The mat draws electrons from the ground into your body, mimicking the effect of walking barefoot on the Earth.
- **Earthing sheets and pillowcases:** For those seeking the benefits of earthing while they sleep, sheets and pillowcases embedded with conductive threads can be a game-changer. These bedding items are connected to the Earth via a grounding cord; when you lie on them, your body absorbs energy from the Earth throughout the night.
- **Earthing bands and patches:** These wearable devices can be attached to your skin at various points, such as the wrists, ankles, or over specific areas of pain. A wire connects them to a grounding point. They are handy for targeted earthing, allowing you to focus on specific areas of the body that may need attention.
- **Earthing shoes:** Innovations in footwear now allow you to stay grounded even while wearing shoes. Earthing shoes are designed with conductive materials in the sole, ensuring that you maintain an electrical connection to the Earth as you walk. They are a practical solution for those who want to practice earthing while doing their daily activities.

When using any earthing equipment, it's essential to ensure that the grounding connection is established and maintained. This typically involves a cord that plugs into a grounded outlet or a grounding rod system. It's crucial to test the outlet with a grounding checker before use in regions with electrical systems that may not be reliably grounded.

Additionally, the maintenance of earthing equipment is straightforward but necessary. Keeping the conductive surfaces clean and free from oils, sweat, and other substances that could interfere with conductivity is essential. Washing instructions vary by product, so follow the manufacturer's guidelines to preserve the effectiveness of your earthing items.

It's worth noting that while earthing equipment can be highly beneficial, like the commercialisation of any health field, they can sometimes be accompanied by unsupported marketing claims which purport false benefits. Remember that such products should complement, not replace, direct contact with the Earth. Aim to integrate barefoot earthing into your routine to embrace the grounding experience naturally and fully.

As we conclude this section, we prepare to navigate the concrete jungles where direct contact with the Earth's surface is less accessible. In the following section, we will explore strategies to stay grounded amidst the hustle and bustle of city life.

Grounding in Different Environments: Urban, Suburban, and Wild

In the grand tapestry of life, we find ourselves woven into a myriad of environments. From the bustling heart of the city to the tranquil suburbs and even the untamed wilderness, each setting offers unique opportunities for grounding. The art of grounding is not confined to any one place; it is a practice that can be embraced wherever you find yourself.

The challenge lies in finding pockets of nature amidst the concrete jungle in urban environments. Yet, within these urban environments, the grounding connection to our planet may yield the most profound benefits, offering a respite from the electromagnetic chaos and the frenetic pace of city living. Parks, community gardens, and even tree-lined streets can serve as grounding sanctuaries. Walking barefoot on grass, hugging a tree, or simply sitting on a park bench with your hands touching the earth can help you connect with the planet's energy. Even in the most built-up areas, the Earth's energy pulses beneath us, waiting to be tapped.

Container gardening can serve as a dual-purpose activity if you have access to private outdoor spaces such as balconies or patios. Gardening is a wonderful grounding activity, allowing you to touch the earth and nurture life physically. Tending to plants and digging in the soil with your bare hands can be a grounding experience, literally and metaphorically. This practice brings you closer to the Earth and fosters a sense of presence and mindfulness. Even a small herb garden can provide an opportunity to touch the Earth through the medium of soil.

Suburban settings often provide more green spaces for grounding. Your backyard can be a grounding haven. Even a simple daily routine of walking barefoot in your yard or sitting on your porch with your feet on the ground can help you absorb the Earth's energy.

In the wild, grounding takes on a more profound dimension. Here, you are in direct contact with the raw, unfiltered energy of the Earth. Whether hiking in the mountains, camping in the forest, or walking along a beach, every step you take barefoot, every moment you spend in contact with the natural world, deepens your grounding experience.

Engaging with water can be another effective form of earthing. Many urban areas feature rivers, lakes, or coastal lines. Taking the time to wade in or touch these water bodies can help ground you. Water is a natural conductor of electricity; thus, it can facilitate the transfer of electrons from the Earth to the body.

Remember, grounding is not just about physical contact with the earth. It's also about mindfulness, being present in the moment, and acknowledging our connection with the larger ecosystem. Whether in a city apartment, a suburban home, or a cabin in the woods, take time each day to ground yourself. Feel the earth beneath you, visualize its energy flowing into you, and let it anchor you in the here and now. Remember that no matter where you are, the earth is always beneath you, ready to offer its grounding energy. Embrace it.

Techniques for Daily Grounding: Incorporating Earthing into Your Routine

As we navigate the concrete jungles of our urban environments, it's easy to feel disconnected from the Earth's natural energy. Yet, the desire to reconnect has never been more palpable. Earthing offers a bridge to this essential connection, promising a host of health benefits we explored in the previous chapter. Now, let's focus on seamlessly integrating earthing into your daily routine.

In the Morning

As the sun peeks over the horizon, painting the sky with hues of orange and pink, the world awakens. This is the perfect time to start your grounding journey. Begin your day with intention. Upon waking, take a moment to step outside, allowing the soles of your feet to make contact with the dew-kissed grass or the cool, moist soil.

The morning dew on the grass is not just a beautiful sight but a conduit for the Earth's energy. Walking barefoot on the dew-kissed grass is a simple yet effective grounding technique. Feel the cool wetness on your feet and the softness of the grass, and let the Earth's energy flow into you. This practice, known as 'dew walking,' is a wonderful way to start your day, aligning your body's energy with the Earth's. This simple act can help set a grounded tone for the day ahead. If you have a garden or backyard, consider creating a small barefoot path with stones, grass, or sand to enhance this morning ritual.

During the Day

As the day progresses, take short grounding breaks. If you work in an office, take a break to step outside, remove your shoes, and place your feet on the ground. If you're at home, step outside and connect with the Earth. Even a few minutes of grounding can help reset your energy and reduce stress.

During lunch, consider eating outside. Eating is inherently grounding, connecting us to the Earth's bounty. By eating outdoors, you can enhance this connection. Feel the sun on your skin, the breeze in your hair, and the Earth beneath you as you nourish your body.

In the Evening

In the evening, grounding can help you do the same as the world begins to wind down. A walk in nature, if accessible, can be an excellent way to end the day. A park or tree-lined street can provide a grounding experience if you live in an urban environment. Pay attention to the sensation of the ground beneath your feet, the rustling of leaves in the wind, and the chirping of birds returning to their nests. These simple observations help you connect with the Earth and ground your energy.

Before bed, consider a grounding meditation. Visualize roots growing from your feet, reaching deep into the Earth, anchoring you. Feel the Earth's energy flowing up these roots, filling your body with calm and stability. This practice can help you release the day's stress and prepare for a restful night's sleep.

Other Ways to Embrace Earthing

Make earthing a family affair. Encourage your loved ones to join you in grounding activities. This could be as simple as walking barefoot in the park together or as engaging as a family gardening project. Not only does this promote health and well-being for everyone involved, but it also strengthens your collective bond with nature and each other.

Travel with grounding in mind. When you're on the road, seek opportunities to connect with the Earth. This could be a walk on the beach, a hike in the forest, or simply finding a patch of grass in a rest area. Portable grounding mats and bands are also available when direct contact with the Earth isn't possible.

For those who enjoy physical activity, consider grounding exercises such as yoga or Tai Chi performed outdoors on the earth's surface. These practices combine the benefits of movement, mindfulness, and grounding in a powerful synergy that can enhance your physical and mental health.

Lastly, practice mindfulness with earthing. As you ground yourself, be present in the moment. Feel the texture of the Earth beneath your feet, the temperature, the moisture. Breathe deeply and acknowledge the subtle energies at play. This mindfulness aspect can enhance the Earthing experience, creating a meditative practice that nurtures both body and soul.

Grounding is not a one-size-fits-all practice. It is a personal journey that you can tailor to your lifestyle and needs. The key is to be mindful, present, and connect with the Earth in a way that feels right for you. By incorporating grounding techniques into your daily routine, from morning to night, you're reconnecting with the Earth's natural rhythms and investing in your long-term well-being.

The Path Forward with Grounding Practices

As we draw this exploration of grounding to a close, it is essential to remember that the journey towards embracing the Earth's energy is not a destination but a continuous process. The path forward with grounding practices is not a straight line but a winding trail that meanders through the landscapes of our daily lives, inviting us to pause, connect, and immerse ourselves in the natural world.

In holistic health, grounding is a gentle yet powerful tool, a bridge that connects us to the Earth and ourselves. It is a practice that invites us to slow down, feel the Earth beneath our feet, and listen to life's subtle rhythms. It is a reminder that we are not separate from the world around us but rather a part of it, woven into the very fabric of life.

The Earth beneath our feet pulses with a natural energy, a gentle current that hums with life and vitality. This energy, often overlooked in our modern, fast-paced lives, has the potential to nourish and rejuvenate us in ways we are only beginning to understand. Grounding allows us to tap into this reservoir of vitality, to draw strength and serenity from the very soil we walk upon.

Incorporating earthing into your daily life does not require drastic changes. It is about making small, mindful adjustments, about taking moments to disconnect from the artificial and reconnect with the natural. It is about grounding your mind in the present, in the tangible reality of the earth beneath your feet. And in doing so, you may find a path to greater mental well-being, a sense of calm and balance rooted in the earth itself.

Earthing is not merely a technique or a tool but a way of life. It is a conscious choice to engage with the Earth's energy, root ourselves in the present moment, and cultivate a deep connection with the world around us. It is a commitment to nurturing our holistic health and wellness and fostering a sense of balance and harmony within ourselves and the environment.

As we move forward, let us remember that grounding is a journey of discovery that invites us to explore, experiment, and experience. It is a journey that encourages us to step outside our comfort zones, challenge our preconceived notions, and question our assumptions. It is a journey that beckons us to venture into the unknown, to delve into the depths of our being, to unearth the treasures that lie within.

In the end, grounding is not about mastering a technique or achieving a goal. It is about cultivating relationships with the Earth, ourselves, and the world. It is about living in harmony with the natural rhythms of life, about embracing the ebb and flow, the rise and fall, the dance of existence. It is about grounding ourselves in the essence of who we are and what it means to be alive. And in this grounding, we find not only a path forward but a homecoming, a return to our true nature, a return to the Earth.

Chapter Summary

- Barefoot earthing involves making direct contact with the Earth's surface by walking, standing, or sitting barefoot on natural grounds, such as soil, grass, sand, or even concrete, to absorb the Earth's electrons.

- Earthing equipment is designed to provide the benefits of earthing without the need to be outdoors or in direct contact with the ground. Such equipment is particularly useful for those living in urban environments or when going barefoot outside isn't practical or possible.
- Grounding can be practiced in various environments, from urban to suburban to wild. Each setting offers unique opportunities for grounding, from parks in the city to gardening in the suburbs to hiking in the wilderness.
- Grounding can be practiced throughout the day, from walking barefoot on dew-kissed grass in the morning to grounding meditation before bed. These practices can help reset energy, reduce stress, and prepare for a restful night's sleep.
- Practicing mindfulness when grounding can enhance the earthing experience, creating a meditative practice that nurtures both your body and soul.
- By incorporating grounding techniques into your daily routine, you're reconnecting with the Earth's natural rhythms and investing in your long-term well-being.
- The journey towards embracing the Earth's energy is continuous. The path forward with grounding practices is a winding trail that invites us to pause, connect, and immerse ourselves in the natural world.
- Grounding is about cultivating a relationship with the Earth, ourselves, and the world. It is about living in harmony with the natural rhythms of life and grounding ourselves in the essence of who we are.

6

PERSONAL STORIES: TRANSFORMATIVE EXPERIENCES WITH EARTHING

I n the vast tapestry of human experience, stories serve as threads, weaving together the intricate patterns of our lives. They are the vessels that carry our truths, lessons, and wisdom. They are the mirrors that reflect our shared humanity. Personal narratives hold a unique and potent power in the realm of earthing. They illuminate the transformative effects of this simple yet profound practice, grounding us in the tangible reality of our connection with the Earth.

Earthing, the act of making direct physical contact with the surface of the Earth, is a practice as old as humanity itself. Yet, in our modern, technology-driven world, it is a practice that has been largely forgotten, overlooked, or dismissed. But the stories of those who have rediscovered earthing and felt its healing touch tell a different tale. They speak of returning to our roots, reconnection with our natural environment, and rekindling our innate capacity for healing and wholeness.

These narratives are not just stories of personal transformation. They are also stories of awakening, a dawning awareness of our place within the larger web of life. They are stories of healing, of the body's remarkable ability to repair and regenerate itself when given the chance. They are stories of emotional and psychological growth, of finding peace, balance, and resilience in the face of life's challenges. They are stories of spiritual journeys, of a deepening sense of purpose and meaning. And they are stories of community, of the ripple effects of one person's transformation on their relationships and broader social circles.

In this chapter, we will delve into these personal narratives, exploring how earthing has touched and transformed lives. We will journey with individuals as they recount their first encounters with earthing, their experiences of physical recovery, their emotional and psychological transformations, their spiritual awakenings, and the impact of their earthing practice on their relationships and communities.

Through these stories, we will understand the power of earthing as a practice and a way of life. In vivid detail, we will see the potential that lies in each of us to reconnect with the Earth, heal, grow, and transform. And perhaps, in the process, we will be inspired to write our own earthing story.

The Awakening: First Encounters with Earthing

In the stillness of the early morning, as the sun's first rays gently kiss the dew-kissed grass, a profound connection occurs when bare feet touch the Earth. This is the awakening, the first encounter with earthing, a moment that has marked the beginning of a transformative journey for many.

For some, this awakening is a sudden, electrifying jolt, a palpable surge of energy that courses through the body, grounding and invigorating them in ways they had never experienced before. It's as if the Earth, in its silent wisdom, has reached out and touched their soul, sparking a connection that feels as ancient as the planet itself.

For others, the awakening is a slow, gentle unfurling, a gradual realization of the subtle shifts occurring within their bodies and minds. It's a soft whisper in the wind, a soothing lullaby sung by the rustling leaves, a comforting embrace that wraps around them, seeping into their bones, blood, and being. It's a sense of coming home, being cradled by the Earth, being part of something larger, something timeless.

These first encounters with earthing are as diverse as the individuals who experience them, yet they all share a common thread - a profound sense of connection and transformation. They speak of a newfound awareness, a deep-seated respect for the Earth and its healing powers, and a sense of peace and balance that permeates every aspect of their lives.

Take, for instance, the story of a middle-aged woman, a corporate executive, who stumbled upon earthing during a wellness retreat. Her first encounter was nothing short of a revelation. As she stood barefoot on the dewy grass, she felt a surge of energy, a sense of calmness washing over her like a gentle wave. It was a moment of pure, unadulterated connection that marked the beginning of her journey towards holistic healing and wellness.

Or consider the tale of a young man, a college student battling anxiety and depression, who discovered earthing through a friend. His first experience was subtle, almost invisible. Yet, over time, he noticed a shift, a gradual easing of his anxiety, a sense of peace that seemed to radiate from the ground beneath his feet. It was a slow awakening, a gentle nudge toward healing and self-discovery.

These stories, and countless others, serve as powerful testaments to the transformative potential of earthing. They remind us of the profound connection we share with the Earth, a connection that has the power to heal, transform, and awaken the deepest parts of our being.

The Healing Ground: Stories of Physical Recovery through Earthing

In the grand tapestry of life, the Earth beneath our feet often goes unnoticed, yet it holds a profound potential for healing. This section is a testament to the transformative power of earthing, as told through the personal narratives of those who have experienced physical recovery through this practice.

Our first story is that of Sarah, a marathon runner from Colorado. A stress fracture had sidelined her, causing not only physical pain but also a deep sense of frustration and loss. It was during this period of recovery that she discovered earthing. Sarah began to spend time barefoot in her garden, allowing the soles of her feet to connect with the cool, damp Earth. She described the sensation as a gentle, grounding energy that seemed to flow into her, soothing her pain and calming her restless spirit.

Over time, her fracture healed, but more than that, she found a new sense of balance and connection.

Then there is James, a retired teacher from Maine, who suffered from chronic insomnia. Nights were long, lonely vigils until he started earthing. He began with simple walks on the beach, feeling the wet sand beneath his feet, the rhythmic pulse of the ocean echoing in his heartbeat. Gradually, his sleep patterns normalized. He attributed this change to the Earth's natural frequencies, which he believed helped regulate his body's rhythms.

In the heart of New York City, we find Maya, a corporate executive who was diagnosed with hypertension. The frenetic pace of her life seemed to echo in her racing heart until she found solace in a small city park. She started spending her lunch breaks there, sitting barefoot on the grass, feeling the steady, reassuring presence of the Earth beneath her. Over time, her blood pressure readings normalized. She felt a sense of calm she hadn't experienced in years.

These stories, and many others, paint a vivid picture of the healing potential of earthing. They show us that the Earth, in its silent, enduring way, offers us a sanctuary of healing and recovery. It invites us to step off the concrete, feel the soil, grass, and sand beneath our feet, and tap into the restorative power that lies beneath the surface.

The following sections will explore the emotional, psychological, and spiritual transformations brought about by earthing. As we delve deeper into these personal narratives, we will discover that the healing ground is not just about physical recovery. It is about reconnecting with our natural environment and rediscovering our place. It is about grounding ourselves in the present moment and finding harmony within ourselves and the world around us.

The Earth's Embrace: Emotional and Psychological Transformations

At the heart of our narrative journey, we delve into the profound emotional and psychological transformations that earthing can initiate. In its infinite wisdom and quiet strength, the Earth can cradle us in its embrace, offering solace and healing to our weary souls.

The stories in this section are as varied as the individuals who share them. Yet, they all speak of a deep, almost primal connection to the Earth that transcends the physical, reaching into the very core of our emotional and psychological being.

One such narrative is that of Nina, a woman who had been grappling with anxiety and depression for most of her adult life. Traditional therapies and medications provided temporary relief, but the darkness always found a way to creep back in. It was only when she discovered earthing that she experienced a profound shift.

Walking barefoot in her garden, feeling the cool, damp soil beneath her feet, Nins felt a sense of calm she hadn't experienced in years. The Earth, she said, absorbed her anxiety, her fears, and her sadness like a sponge soaking up water. Over time, her connection with the Earth became her sanctuary and healing place. The Earth's embrace became her therapy, grounding her emotions and thoughts and allowing her to experience life with a newfound sense of peace and balance.

Then there's the story of Ryan, a war veteran haunted by the ghosts of his past. His companions were nightmares, flashbacks, and a constant sense of unease until he stumbled upon earthing. The simple act of standing barefoot on the Earth, feeling its steady pulse beneath his feet, began to soothe his troubled mind. The Earth, he said, didn't judge or demand; it simply was. This acceptance, this unconditional embrace, allowed him to process his trauma and find a semblance of peace amidst the chaos.

These stories, and countless others, illustrate the profound emotional and psychological transformations that earthing can facilitate. They remind us that we are not separate from the Earth but intrinsically connected to it. And in this connection, in the Earth's quiet, unassuming embrace, we can find healing, peace, and transformation.

The Harmonious Connection: Spiritual Journeys Initiated by Earthing

In the heart of our existence lies a profound longing for connection, a yearning to be part of something greater than ourselves. This longing often leads us on spiritual journeys, quests for meaning and purpose that transcend the mundane and the material. For many, earthing has catalyzed such journeys, opening up new pathways of understanding and experience that resonate deeply with the soul.

The stories in this section are a testament to the transformative power of earthing on a spiritual level. They are tales of individuals who have discovered a sense of unity and harmony that extends beyond the physical realm through their direct contact with the Earth.

One such story is that of Beth, a woman in her mid-thirties who had spent most of her life feeling disconnected and adrift. Despite her successful career and seemingly perfect life, she felt an emptiness within that she couldn't quite understand. It was only when she stumbled upon the practice of earthing during a wellness retreat that she experienced a profound shift.

Walking barefoot on the dew-kissed grass, she felt a surge of energy coursing through her, a sensation she described as "coming home." This was not just a physical sensation but a spiritual awakening. She felt a deep sense of belonging, a connection to the Earth and the universe she had never experienced before.

In the silence of the early morning, with the Earth beneath her feet and the sky above her, Beth found a sense of peace and wholeness that had eluded her for years. She began to see herself not as an isolated entity but as an integral part of the web of life. This realization sparked a spiritual journey that transformed her life, leading her to a deeper understanding of herself and her place in the world.

Beth's story is not an isolated one. Many others have embarked on similar spiritual journeys initiated by earthing, finding in practice a bridge between the physical and the spiritual, the self and the universe. They have discovered a harmonious connection that has enriched their lives, bringing peace, purpose, and profound joy.

In the grand tapestry of existence, we are all interconnected threads woven together by the energy of the Earth. Through earthing, we can tap into this energy, grounding ourselves in the present moment and opening ourselves up to the spiritual dimensions of our being. As these personal stories illustrate, the journey may be deeply personal, but the destination is universal: a harmonious connection with the Earth, ourselves, and the cosmos.

The Ripple Effect: How Earthing Transformed Relationships and Communities

The practice of earthing is not an isolated phenomenon. It ripples out, touching the individual and the relationships and communities around them. This section explores the transformative power of earthing as it extends beyond the self, reshaping relationships and revitalizing communities.

The stories shared here are as diverse as the people who tell them, yet they all echo a common theme: earthing has a profound capacity to foster connection. It begins personally with the individual forming a deep, grounding bond with the Earth. This connection, in turn, influences their interactions with others.

Consider the story of Marianne, a mother of two from Colorado. She discovered earthing during a period of personal turmoil. As she began to spend time barefoot in her garden, she noticed a shift in her mood and energy levels. This newfound calm and vitality had a ripple effect on her family life. Inspired by her example, her children began to join her in the garden. The shared experience of earthing brought them closer, fostering a sense of unity and mutual understanding that had been missing in their relationship.

Similarly, a community found unity through earthing in the small coastal town of Astoria, Oregon. Once a neglected space, the local park became a hub for earthing enthusiasts. As more people began to gather, barefoot and open-hearted, the park transformed into a vibrant community space. The practice of earthing became a shared language, bridging gaps between generations and backgrounds. It fostered a sense of belonging, a connection to the Earth and each other.

These stories illuminate the transformative power of earthing as it ripples outwards, touching relationships and communities. They remind us that earthing is not just a solitary practice but a collective experience. It is a shared journey of grounding, healing, and connection. As we connect with the Earth, we also connect with each other, creating a profound ripple effect that can transform our relationships and communities.

In the next section, we will reflect on the personal and collective impact of earthing, drawing together the threads of these personal narratives to understand the broader implications of this practice.

Reflecting on the Personal and Collective Impact of Earthing

As we draw this chapter close, we find ourselves standing on the precipice of understanding, looking out over the vast spectrum of personal and collective transformation that earthing has brought about. The stories we've shared are tales of individual awakening, healing, and spiritual growth, as well as narratives of community bonding and societal change.

Earthing, as we've seen, is not merely a practice. It is a way of life, a philosophy that encourages us to reconnect with the natural world, ground ourselves in the Earth's energy, and find balance and harmony within ourselves and others. The personal impact of earthing is profound, as evidenced by the stories of physical recovery, emotional healing, and spiritual awakening.

But the power of earthing extends beyond the individual. It ripples outwards, touching those around us, transforming relationships, and fostering community. It encourages us to slow down, be present, and listen to our bodies, the Earth beneath our feet, and the people around us. It teaches us to respect and care for the natural world, to recognize our place within it, and to understand that our health and well-being are intrinsically linked to the health and well-being of the planet.

The collective impact of earthing is best seen in the growing movement towards sustainable living and environmental stewardship. As more and more people discover the benefits of earthing, they are also becoming more aware of the need to protect and preserve the natural world. This shift in consciousness is leading to changes in behavior, from the choices we make as consumers to the policies we support as citizens.

In reflecting on the personal and collective impact of earthing, we are reminded of the interconnectedness of all things. We are part of the Earth, and the Earth is part of us. Our stories are woven into the fabric of the planet, and the planet's story is woven into us. Through earthing, we are grounding ourselves physically, emotionally, psychologically, and spiritually. We are finding our place in the world, and in doing so, we are helping to shape a more balanced, harmonious, and sustainable future.

Chapter Summary

- Personal narratives illuminate the profound, transformative effects of earthing, which involves making direct physical contact with the Earth. These stories highlight this practice's healing and grounding effects, which are largely overlooked in our modern, technology-driven world.
- First encounters with earthing can be powerful and transformative, sparking a deep connection with the Earth that can be refreshing and calming. These experiences often mark the beginning of a journey towards holistic healing and wellness.
- Earthing has the potential to aid physical recovery. Stories of individuals who have experienced healing from conditions like stress fractures, insomnia, and hypertension through earthing underscore the Earth's restorative power.
- The practice of earthing can facilitate profound emotional and psychological transformations. Earthing can help individuals find peace, balance, and healing by grounding their emotions and thoughts.
- Earthing can initiate spiritual journeys, fostering a sense of unity and harmony that extends beyond the physical realm. Through earthing, individuals can experience a deep sense of belonging and connection to the universe.
- The practice of earthing can have a ripple effect, transforming not only the individual but also their relationships and

communities. Shared experiences of earthing can foster unity, mutual understanding, and a sense of belonging.

- The collective impact of earthing is seen in the growing movement towards sustainable living and environmental stewardship. As more people discover the benefits of earthing, they become more aware of the need to protect and preserve the natural world.
- The personal and collective impact of earthing reminds us of the interconnectedness of all things. Through earthing, we are grounding ourselves physically, emotionally, psychologically, and spiritually, helping to shape a more balanced, harmonious, and sustainable future.

7

EARTHING ACROSS CULTURES: A GLOBAL PERSPECTIVE

E
arthing is a universal language, spoken not in words but in the silent communion between the soles of our feet and the soil beneath them. This language transcends geographical boundaries, cultural differences, and historical epochs, uniting us all in a shared experience of the Earth's grounding energy.

In its infinite wisdom, the Earth has been whispering to us since the dawn of time. It has been telling us stories of life and death, growth and decay, and the eternal cycle of seasons. It has taught us balance, harmony, resilience and regeneration. And it has been inviting us to join this grand symphony of life, to become active participants in the unfolding drama of the natural world.

Earthing is our response to this invitation. It is our way of saying 'yes' to the Earth, acknowledging our place in the grand scheme of things, and embracing our role as stewards of this beautiful planet. It is our way of tuning into the Earth's frequency, aligning our rhythms with the rhythms of nature, and grounding ourselves in the here and now.

Earthing is not a new concept nor exclusive to any particular culture or tradition. It is a universal practice rooted in our shared human experience. From the indigenous tribes of the Amazon rainforest to the nomadic herders of the Mongolian steppes, from the yogis of ancient

India to the philosophers of classical Greece, from the shamans of Africa to the scientists of the modern West, people from all walks of life and all corners of the globe have been practicing earthing in one form or another.

This chapter will take you on a journey around the world, exploring how different cultures have interpreted and practiced earthing. It will delve into the deep-rooted connection between indigenous cultures and the Earth, the Eastern philosophies that view earthing as a way of harnessing the energy of life, the Western scientific approach to earthing, and the African traditions that see earthing as a spiritual practice. It will also look at the modern revival of earthing and what the future might hold for this ancient practice.

So, let's embark on this journey together, exploring the universal language of earthing and discovering how it can help us connect with the Earth, each other, and ourselves.

Earthing in Indigenous Cultures: A Deep-rooted Connection

In the heart of the world's most ancient cultures, the practice of earthing, or grounding, is not a novelty or a trend but a way of life deeply woven into their existence. Indigenous cultures, from the Aboriginal tribes of Australia to the Native Americans of North America, have long recognized the Earth as a living entity, a source of life, and a conduit for healing and spiritual connection.

For instance, the Aboriginal people of Australia have a profound relationship with the land that transcends the physical. Their Dreamtime stories speak of the Earth as a sacred mother, a provider, and a spiritual guide. Walking barefoot on the Earth, sleeping on the ground, and participating in ceremonies that connect them to the land are integral parts of their culture. This intimate connection with the Earth, this practice of earthing, is believed to maintain their physical health and spiritual well-being and to keep them in harmony with the cycles of nature.

Similarly, Native American cultures have a rich tradition of earthing. The Earth is revered as a powerful spiritual entity, and many rituals and ceremonies involve direct contact with the Earth. Sweat lodges, for example, are built directly on the Earth, and participants sit on the ground inside, connecting with the Earth's energy as they purify and heal. The practice of earthing is also evident in their daily life, from walking barefoot to sleeping on the Earth.

In these cultures, earthing is not merely a physical act but a holistic practice encompassing the body, mind, and spirit. It is a way of grounding oneself in the present, connecting with the energy of life that pulses beneath our feet, and acknowledging our place in the vast web of life that the Earth supports.

Though varied in their specifics, these indigenous practices of earthing share a common understanding: that the Earth is a source of healing, energy, and spiritual connection. They remind us that we are not separate from the Earth but a part of it and that by connecting with the Earth, we connect with ourselves and the greater whole. As we delve deeper into the practice of earthing, we find that this ancient wisdom holds profound relevance for our modern lives, offering a path to health, balance, and a more profound sense of connection with the world around us.

Eastern Philosophies: Earthing and the Energy of Life

In the East, the concept of earthing and grounding is not novel. It is deeply embedded in their philosophies and way of life, intertwined with the fundamental principles of energy and balance. The Eastern philosophies, particularly those of China, India, and Japan, have long recognized the Earth as a source of life-giving energy, a conduit for healing, and a medium for spiritual connection.

In Chinese philosophy, 'Qi' or 'Chi' is central. It is the life force or energy flow that permeates everything in the universe. In this context, the Earth is seen as a reservoir of this vital energy. Walking barefoot, practicing Tai Chi in nature, or meditating outdoors are ways to connect with the Earth's energy, balance one's Qi, and promote physical and emotional well-being.

Similarly, in Indian philosophy, the Earth is revered as 'Prithvi' or 'Bhumi,' the goddess of the Earth. The practice of yoga, particularly

'Hatha Yoga,' encourages a deep connection with the Earth. The term 'Hatha' combines 'Ha,' meaning sun, and 'Tha,' meaning moon, symbolizing the balance of energies. Many yoga asanas or postures are designed to ground the practitioner, to help them draw energy from the Earth, and to create a harmonious flow of life force or 'Prana' within.

In Japan, the practice of 'Shinrin-yoku' or 'forest bathing' is a testament to the Japanese belief in the healing power of nature. It is a practice of immersing oneself in the forest, of connecting with the Earth through all five senses. The Earth, the trees, and the air are all seen as sources of 'Ki,' the universal energy.

These Eastern philosophies, with their emphasis on the energy of life, offer a holistic approach to earthing. They see the Earth not just as a physical entity but as a spiritual and energetic one. They recognize that our relationship with the Earth is not merely physical but deeply energetic and spiritual. They teach us that by grounding ourselves and connecting with the Earth, we can balance our energies, enhance our well-being, and deepen our understanding of ourselves and the universe.

In the next section, we will explore the Western perspectives on earthing, where the focus shifts from the spiritual and energetic to the scientific and empirical.

Western Perspectives: The Scientific Approach to Earthing

In the West, the concept of earthing and grounding has been approached with a scientific lens. This perspective, while different from other cultures' spiritual and philosophical interpretations, is no less profound in its implications.

The scientific exploration of earthing began in earnest in the late 20th century, with researchers seeking to understand the physiological effects of direct physical contact with the Earth's surface. The Earth, they discovered, is a vast reservoir of negatively charged free electrons. When a human body makes direct contact with the Earth, these electrons are absorbed, stabilizing the body's bioelectrical environment, as we learned in earlier chapters.

This discovery led to a series of studies examining the potential health benefits of earthing. The results were intriguing. Regular grounding, researchers found, could reduce inflammation, improve sleep, increase energy, lower stress, and enhance the body's healing processes. These findings provided a scientific basis for the intuitive wisdom of indigenous cultures, who have long recognized the Earth's healing power.

Yet, the Western approach to earthing is not without its critics. Some argue that the focus on physiological benefits overlooks the practice's deeper, more holistic aspects. Earthing, they contend, is not just about absorbing electrons but about reconnecting with the natural world, grounding oneself in the present moment, and fostering a sense of belonging to the more extensive web of life.

Despite these debates, the scientific exploration of earthing has played a crucial role in its global resurgence. It has brought the practice into the mainstream, sparking interest among health professionals, wellness enthusiasts, and the general public. It has also opened up new avenues for research, with scientists now investigating the potential of earthing to treat various health conditions, from chronic pain to cardiovascular disease.

Ultimately, the Western perspective on earthing offers a compelling blend of ancient wisdom and modern science. It reminds us that, despite our technological advances, we are still creatures of the Earth, bound by its rhythms and sustained by its energies. And it invites us to explore this connection, not just as a path to better health but as a way of living more fully, consciously, and harmoniously with the world around us.

African Traditions: Earthing as a Spiritual Practice

In Africa's vast and diverse continent, the practice of earthing and grounding is not merely a physical act but a spiritual journey. It is a sacred ritual, a conduit for connecting with the ancestors, the Earth, and the divine. The African perspective on earthing is deeply rooted in the belief that the Earth is a living, breathing entity, a source of life and wisdom, and a spiritual guide.

In many African cultures, the Earth is revered as a mother figure, a nurturing entity that provides sustenance, protection, and wisdom. The act of earthing and making direct contact with the Earth is seen as a way of tapping into this wisdom, of drawing strength and guidance from the Earth. It is a practice often incorporated into spiritual rituals and ceremonies, grounding the participants and connecting them with the spiritual realm.

In the Yoruba culture of West Africa, for instance, the Earth is personified as the goddess Ile, the mother of all beings. Ile is revered as a source of wisdom and guidance, and the act of earthing is seen as a way of communing with her, of seeking her counsel. During spiritual ceremonies, participants often touch the Earth, a symbolic act of reaching out to Ile and seeking her blessing and guidance.

Similarly, in the Zulu culture of South Africa, the Earth is seen as a spiritual entity, a source of life and wisdom. The act of earthing is incorporated into many spiritual rituals, connecting with the ancestors and seeking their guidance and protection. It is a practice deeply ingrained in the culture, a testament to the enduring connection between the people and the Earth.

In these cultures, and many others across the continent, earthing is not merely a physical act but a spiritual practice, a way of connecting with the divine, seeking guidance and wisdom. It is a practice deeply rooted in the culture, a testament to the enduring connection between the people and the Earth.

As we explore the practice of earthing across cultures, it becomes clear that it is more than just a physical act. It is a spiritual journey, a way of connecting with the Earth, the divine, and ourselves. It is a practice that transcends cultural boundaries, a universal language that speaks to our innate need for connection, grounding, and a sense of belonging. It is a practice that remains, at its core, a shared ground despite its many interpretations and manifestations.

Global Trends: The Modern Revival of Earthing

A quiet revolution is taking place in the heart of our technologically driven world. It is a movement that is not about advancing further into the digital age but rather about returning to our roots, to the Earth beneath our feet. This is the modern revival of earthing, a global trend reconnecting individuals with the natural world.

The modern revival of earthing is not a sudden phenomenon. It is a gradual awakening, a slow but steady realization of the importance of our connection with the Earth. It is a response to the increasing disconnection we feel in our fast-paced, urbanized lives, where concrete and screens often replace grass and skies.

This trend is not confined to any one region or culture. From the bustling cities of Tokyo and New York to the tranquil countryside of Tuscany and the rugged landscapes of Australia, people are rediscovering the grounding effects of direct contact with the Earth. They walk barefoot in parks, practice yoga on the beach, garden with their hands, and sleep on earthing sheets. They are seeking out these experiences not just for the physical benefits but also for the mental and emotional balance they bring.

A growing body of scientific research also fuels the modern revival of earthing. Studies reveal the potential impact of earthing on everything from sleep quality and stress levels to inflammation and pain management. This scientific validation is helping to bridge the gap between ancient wisdom and modern understanding, making earthing more accessible and appealing to a broader audience.

But perhaps the most powerful driver of this trend is the personal experiences of those who practice earthing. The stories of transformation and healing, peace and clarity inspire others to try earthing for themselves. They prove that in a constantly changing and evolving world, some things remain constant. The Earth beneath our feet is one of them.

As we look to the future, the modern revival of earthing shows no signs of slowing down. It is a testament to our innate need for connection, not just with each other but with the Earth itself. It is a reminder that no matter where we come from or where we are going, we all share the same ground. And that is a powerful message in a world that can often feel divided.

The Future of Earthing - A Shared Ground

As we draw this global exploration of earthing to a close, we find ourselves standing on a shared ground, a common soil that binds us all, regardless of our cultural, geographical, or philosophical differences. The future of earthing is a future of unity and shared understanding, a future where the wisdom of the ancients meets the discoveries of modern science and where the spiritual meets the physical in a harmonious dance of energy and connection.

The resurgence of earthing in contemporary society is a testament to our innate longing for connection, not just with each other but with the natural world surrounding and sustaining us. As we move forward, this connection will guide us, grounding us in the wisdom of the Earth and the energy of life itself.

In the West, scientific research continues to uncover the tangible benefits of earthing, validating what indigenous cultures and Eastern philosophies have known for centuries. The Earth's energy profoundly impacts our physical and mental well-being. As we continue to explore this connection, we can expect to see a greater emphasis on earthing in health and wellness.

In Africa, the spiritual practice of earthing continues to thrive, reminding us of the deep-rooted connection between the Earth and the human spirit. As we look to the future, we can expect to see a greater integration of these spiritual practices into the global conversation on earthing, enriching our understanding and deepening our connection to the Earth.

Across the globe, the practice of earthing is being revived, reimagined, and reintegrated into our daily lives. From the forests of North America to the deserts of Africa, from the mountains of Asia to the plains of Australia, people are rediscovering the power of earthing and, in doing so, are rediscovering a part of themselves.

The future of earthing is a shared ground, a common soil that unites us in our diversity and reminds us of our shared humanity. As we move forward, let us do so with our feet firmly planted on the Earth, our hearts open to the wisdom of the ancients, and our minds attuned to the discoveries of the present. In this balance, this harmonious dance of energy and connection, we will find our true grounding.

Chapter Summary

- Earthing, or grounding, is a universal practice that involves direct contact with the Earth's natural energy. It transcends geographical boundaries and cultural differences, uniting us all in a shared experience of the Earth's grounding energy.
- Indigenous cultures, such as the Aboriginal tribes of Australia and the Native Americans, have a deep-rooted connection with the Earth. They view the Earth as a living entity, a source of life, healing, and spiritual connection.
- Eastern philosophies, particularly those of China, India, and Japan, view the Earth as a source of life-giving energy. Practices like Tai Chi, Yoga, and Shinrin-yoku are seen as ways to connect with the Earth's energy and balance one's life force.
- In the West, the concept of earthing has been approached scientifically. Research has shown that regular grounding can reduce inflammation, improve sleep, increase energy, lower stress, and enhance the body's healing processes.
- African traditions view earthing as a spiritual practice. The Earth is seen as a spiritual entity, a source of life and wisdom, and earthing is often incorporated into spiritual rituals and ceremonies.
- The modern revival of earthing is a global trend driven by a growing body of scientific research and personal experiences of transformation and healing. People are rediscovering the grounding effects of direct contact with the Earth, seeking mental and emotional balance and physical benefits.
- The future of earthing lies in a shared understanding and unity. The wisdom of the ancients meets the discoveries of modern science, and the spiritual meets the physical in a harmonious dance of energy and connection.

- The resurgence of earthing in contemporary society is a testament to our innate longing for connection with the natural world. As we move forward, this connection will guide us, grounding us in the wisdom of the Earth and the energy of life itself.

8

EARTHING AND ENVIRONMENTAL HEALTH

As we delve deeper into earthing and grounding, it becomes
evident that the simple act of connecting with the Earth's
surface extends beyond personal health benefits and touches
upon a broader, more profound aspect of our existence: ecological awareness. At its core, earthing is an invitation to rekindle our relationship with
the natural world. This relationship for many has been disturbed by the
walls of modern living and the screens of digital devices.

Ecological awareness is rooted in the understanding that we are not
separate entities from our environment but interconnected parts of a vast
ecosystem. When we walk barefoot on the grass, stand under a tree's
stretching branches, and immerse our hands in the rich, damp soil, we
engage in a silent dialogue with the Earth. This dialogue is a reminder of
the delicate balance that sustains all life on Earth.

Through the practice of earthing, we become more attuned to the
delicate rhythms of nature. We start to notice the subtle changes in the
quality of the air, the moisture in the soil, and the vibrancy of the plants
around us. We develop a greater appreciation for the natural world and a
stronger yearning to protect it. After all, the well-being of our planet is
inextricably linked to our own.

Earthing encourages us to consider the impact of our actions on the environment. As we become more aware of the connectivity we share with the Earth, we may also grow more conscious of the activities that our modern lifestyles entail.

This awareness can inspire us to make more environmentally conscious choices, such as reducing energy consumption, opting for cleaner energy sources, and minimizing our reliance on technology that contributes to electromagnetic pollution. It can also lead to advocacy for more sustainable practices and policies that protect the Earth's integrity.

In essence, earthing is not just a personal health practice but a pathway to environmental stewardship. We can also ground ourselves philosophically by grounding ourselves physically, developing a more profound respect for the natural world and a commitment to its preservation. This shift in perspective is vital as we face the escalating challenges of climate change, biodiversity loss, and environmental degradation.

In the next section, we will explore how grounding practices can be integrated into a lifestyle that favors ecological balance and sustainability. This integration is beneficial for individual health and the planet's health as we learn to live in greater synergy with the natural world.

Earthing and Sustainable Living

As we delve deeper into the interconnected relationship between earthing and the environment, we realize that the practice of earthing is not just beneficial for our well-being but also the sustainability of our planet. At its core, sustainable living is about making choices that ensure the health and well-being of both the environment and ourselves. Earthing, or grounding, aligns seamlessly with this philosophy by fostering a deeper connection between ourselves and Earth's natural systems.

Sustainable living encourages us to reduce our carbon footprint, conserve resources, and live harmoniously with the natural world. Earthing contributes to this lifestyle by reinforcing the importance of preserving the natural environment that provides this healing energy. When we walk barefoot on the Earth, we are not just receiving energy but also stepping into a relationship with the land that sustains us. This act can heighten our awareness of the land's condition and the impact of our actions upon it.

The practice of earthing can inspire us to adopt eco-friendly habits. For example, spending time in nature may lead to a greater appreciation for its beauty and a stronger desire to protect it. This could result in choices such as using fewer chemicals on our lawns and gardens, which not only allows for better conductivity with the Earth but also reduces the amount of harmful substances that seep into the soil and waterways.

In addition, the materials used for earthing products, such as conductive mats and sheets, can be designed with sustainability in mind. Manufacturers who prioritize eco-friendly production processes and materials help to minimize the environmental impact of these products. By choosing products made with natural and sustainable materials, we can support the environment while reaping the health benefits of grounding.

The principles of earthing can be integrated into the design and construction of eco-friendly homes and communities. By incorporating conductive materials and grounding technologies, these living spaces can be designed to facilitate regular earthing experiences, promoting both environmental health and personal well-being. This approach to architecture and community planning enhances the connection to the Earth and supports the broader goals of sustainable development.

In the context of sustainable living, earthing serves as a reminder of the intricate interdependence between our health and the health of our planet. It encourages us to live with greater environmental consciousness, understanding that the Earth is not merely a backdrop for human activity but a living system that we are a part of and responsible for. As we continue to explore the role of earthing in permaculture in the following section, we will see how these concepts can be practically applied to create self-sustaining and regenerative agricultural practices that honor and harness the Earth's natural energies.

The Role of Earthing in Permaculture

Earthing finds a harmonious partnership in the embrace of permaculture. Permaculture—a contraction of "permanent agriculture"—is a philosophy and approach to land management that adopts arrangements observed in flourishing natural ecosystems. It is a design system characterized by its alignment with the patterns and resilient features of natural ecosystems. Earthing is pivotal in the permaculture ethos, enriching the land and those who tend to it.

At the heart of permaculture lies the principle of caring for the Earth, an ethos that resonates deeply with the practice of earthing. By walking barefoot on the soil, engaging in hands-on gardening, or utilizing grounding technologies, we can experience a direct connection with the Earth. This connection is not merely symbolic; it is a physical bonding that allows for the transfer of electrons from the ground into the body, promoting a sense of well-being and fostering a deeper understanding of the interconnectedness of life.

The role of earthing in permaculture extends beyond the individual to the land itself. Soil health is paramount in permaculture, and grounding practices can influence soil vitality. The Earth's natural electrical charge can affect the microbial life within the soil, which in turn supports plant growth and the overall health of the garden ecosystem. By maintaining a living connection with the ground, permaculture practitioners help ensure that the soil remains vibrant and full of life, essential for sustainable food production and ecological balance.

Moreover, earthing principles can be integrated into permaculture design through the conscious arrangement of plants and structures to enhance the natural energy flow. For instance, the placement of certain conductive plants or the use of water features can create a landscape that supports the ecosystem's health and facilitates grounding for humans and animals alike. This design approach recognizes the Earth as a source of healing energy that can be harnessed to benefit all living beings.

In permaculture, every element is carefully considered for its function and relationship to the whole. Earthing is no exception. It is a practice for individual health and a tool for building resilient and dynamic ecosystems. The grounding of both people and plants can lead to more robust and productive gardens, which in turn contribute to the health of the larger environment.

The integration of earthing into permaculture practices also serves as a reminder of the importance of observing and mimicking natural processes. Just as the Earth maintains a balance through its cycles and systems, permaculture seeks to emulate this balance in its designs, creating sustainable and nurturing spaces. Earthing reinforces this connection, grounding us in the understanding that human and environmental health are inextricably linked.

As we transition to the next section, let us carry the understanding that earthing is not only a personal health practice but also a vital component of environmental stewardship. Grounding ourselves is a tangible way to acknowledge and enhance our relationship with the natural world. This relationship is central to the permaculture philosophy and essential for the health of our planet.

Connecting with Nature for Planetary Health

In the grand tapestry of our planet's health, each thread is interwoven with delicate precision, creating a balance that sustains all life forms. As we delve deeper into the practice of earthing, it becomes increasingly apparent that our connection with the Earth is not merely a pathway to individual well-being but also a vital link to the health of our planet. The Earth's surface is teeming with natural energies that can lead to profound environmental healing when engaged with respect and understanding.

Our planet is a living, breathing entity, and just like any organism, it requires care and nurturing. With its rapid technological advancements and urban sprawl, our modern lifestyle has led to a disconnection from the natural world. This detachment not only affects our health but also contributes to the degradation of the environment. Pollution, deforestation, and the exploitation of natural resources have resulted in a planet in distress. However, by reconnecting with nature through earthing, we can begin to reverse some of these adverse effects.

When we walk barefoot on the Earth, we do more than absorb the beneficial electrons that reduce inflammation and promote health. We also engage in an act of reciprocity with the environment. This practice encourages a greater awareness of the land beneath our feet—the soil that supports plant life, the grasses that feed the insects, and the ecosystems that depend on a delicate balance to thrive. By grounding ourselves, we become more attuned to the natural cycles and the environment's needs, fostering a sense of stewardship for the Earth.

Earthing can inspire a shift in how we interact with our surroundings. It can lead to more sustainable choices, such as adopting organic farming practices that honor the Earth's natural rhythms rather than depleting its resources. It can influence the materials we use, the food we consume, and how we manage waste. Through a grounded connection with the Earth, we can develop a deeper understanding of the impact of our actions and the importance of living in harmony with nature.

The health of our planet is inextricably linked to our own. When we ground ourselves, we not only draw healing energy from the Earth but also contribute to its restoration. Each step taken on the soft soil, each moment spent in contemplation of the natural world, is an opportunity to participate in the healing of our environment. As we nurture our connection with the Earth, we contribute to a collective effort to preserve the planet for future generations.

In this way, earthing transcends the realm of personal health and becomes a catalyst for environmental transformation. It is a practice that reminds us of our inherent connection to all living things and our responsibility to protect the intricate web of life. By grounding ourselves, we can foster a deeper respect for the Earth, leading to actions that support planetary health and ensure the vitality of our shared home.

As we move forward, let us carry with us the understanding that our relationship with the Earth is not one of dominion but of partnership. Through earthing, we can rekindle our bond with nature and work towards a future where the planet's health is seen as a reflection of our own.

Chapter Summary

- Earthing and grounding reconnects us with the Earth, promoting ecological awareness, and reminding us of our interconnectedness with the environment.

- The practice of earthing attunes us to nature's rhythms, fostering a greater appreciation for the natural world and a desire to protect it.
- Earthing encourages environmentally conscious choices and sustainable practices, reducing our ecological footprint and electromagnetic pollution.
- The practice of earthing aligns with the concept of sustainable living, inspiring eco-friendly habits and choices in materials and products.
- Earthing principles can be integrated into eco-friendly architecture and community planning, enhancing environmental health and personal well-being.
- In permaculture, earthing enriches the land and those who tend to it, supporting soil health and the design of resilient ecosystems.
- Earthing in permaculture emphasizes observing natural processes, creating sustainable spaces, and recognizing the link between human and environmental health.
- The practice of earthing is a catalyst for environmental transformation, fostering stewardship for the Earth and encouraging a better contribution to planetary health.

9

THE FUTURE OF EARTHING: TRENDS
AND PREDICTIONS

A s we stand on the precipice of a new era, we find ourselves
drawn back to the Earth, to the grounding energy that pulses
beneath our feet. The journey towards a grounded future is not
a new path but rather a rediscovery of an ancient practice, a return to our
roots. It is a journey that beckons us to shed the shackles of our modern,
disconnected lives and embrace the Earth's healing power.

In recent years, we have seen a resurgence in the popularity of earthing. From the sandy beaches of Australia to the lush forests of Scandinavia, people are rediscovering the benefits of connecting with the Earth.
They feel the Earth's calming, healing energy and seek to incorporate
earthing into their daily lives.

But the journey towards a grounded future is not without its challenges. As we move forward, we must navigate the complexities of our
modern world, from the rapid pace of technological innovation to the
looming threat of climate change. We must find ways to ground ourselves
in urban landscapes, to connect with the Earth even when concrete and
steel stand in our way. We must explore the role of earthing in future
health and wellness trends, understanding how this ancient practice can
contribute to our holistic well-being in the 21st century.

As we embark on this journey, let us remember that the Earth is not just beneath us but within us. It is a part of us, a part of our very being. And as we move towards a grounded future, let us embrace the Earth's energy, our connection to the Earth, and our holistic, grounded selves.

The Rising Popularity of Earthing: A Global Perspective

As the sun rises, painting the sky with hues of orange and pink, a new day begins. Across the globe, from the bustling streets of Tokyo to the serene landscapes of rural Ireland, a quiet revolution is taking place. People are stepping barefoot on the Earth, feeling the cool dew-kissed grass beneath their feet, and connecting with the planet profoundly and primally. This is earthing, a practice as old as humanity itself, yet experiencing a resurgence in popularity that is nothing short of remarkable.

As we grapple with the stress and disconnection of our fast-paced lives, more and more people are turning to earthing to reconnect with nature and restore balance to their bodies and minds.

Earthing is gaining traction around the world. In the United States, a country often seen as the epicenter of modern lifestyle diseases, earthing is being embraced by a diverse range of individuals. Celebrities, athletes, and everyday people are all discovering the benefits of this simple yet powerful practice.

In Europe, the trend is equally evident. From the United Kingdom to Germany, people are increasingly seeking out green spaces to practice earthing, whether it's in city parks, private gardens, or the vast expanses of the countryside. The practice has also found a place in the wellness tourism industry, with retreats and wellness resorts incorporating earthing into their offerings.

With its rich history of holistic healing practices, Asia has also welcomed the earthing movement. In Japan, a country known for its deep respect for nature, earthing is being integrated into traditional practices like forest bathing or shinrin-yoku. In India, the birthplace of yoga, earthing is combined with this ancient practice to create a holistic wellness experience.

The rising popularity of earthing is a testament to our collective desire to reconnect with the Earth and restore balance to our lives. It is a global movement, transcending borders and cultures, uniting us in our shared need for connection and healing. As we look to the future, it is clear that earthing will continue to play a vital role in our journey towards a more grounded, holistic existence.

Technological Innovations in Earthing Practices

As we delve deeper into the future of earthing, it is impossible to over-look the role of technology in shaping and enhancing our connection with the Earth. The marriage of technology and earthing may seem para-doxical since earthing is fundamentally about returning to nature and disconnecting from our increasingly digital world. However, when used thoughtfully and responsibly, technology can be a powerful tool to deepen our understanding of the Earth and its energy and make earthing practices more accessible and practical.

One of the most significant technological innovations in earthing practices is the development of earthing or grounding mats. These devices, which can be placed under your feet or body, are designed to mimic the effects of walking barefoot on the Earth, even when you are indoors. They are connected to the Earth via a wire and a grounded wall outlet, allowing you to tap into its energy from the comfort of your home or office.

Another innovation is the advent of earthing shoes. Unlike traditional footwear, which often insulates us from the Earth, earthing shoes are made with conductive materials that allow the Earth's electrons to flow into our bodies. This means you can stay grounded even when walking on concrete or other artificial surfaces.

The rise of wearable technology has opened up new possibilities for monitoring and enhancing our earthing practices. For instance, some companies are now developing wearable devices that can measure your level of grounding in real time, providing you with immediate feedback and helping you to optimize your earthing experience.

However, as we embrace these technological innovations, it is crucial to remember that they are not replacements for direct contact with the Earth. Instead, they are tools that complement and enrich our earthing practices, especially in urban environments where direct contact with the Earth is often challenging.

In the future, we can expect to see even more technological innovations in earthing practices, driven by ongoing research into the health benefits of earthing and the growing demand for holistic wellness solutions. As we journey towards a more grounded future, technology will undoubtedly play an essential role in helping us to reconnect with the Earth and harness its healing energy.

The Impact of Climate Change on Earthing

As we delve deeper into the future of earthing, we cannot ignore the looming specter of climate change. This global phenomenon, characterized by rising temperatures, erratic weather patterns, and a general disruption of natural ecosystems, has far-reaching implications for our relationship with the Earth.

Climate change, in its essence, is a disruption of the Earth's natural rhythms. It is a dissonance in the symphony of nature, a discord that reverberates through every aspect of our lives. As practitioners and advocates of earthing, we must acknowledge and address this disruption.

Earthing, at its core, is about connection. It is about grounding ourselves in the Earth's natural energy, tapping into the planet's primal pulse. But what happens when that pulse is disrupted? What happens when the rhythms we rely on become erratic and unpredictable?

The impact of climate change on earthing is multidimensional. On a physical level, changes in weather patterns can make it more challenging to practice earthing. Increased temperatures can make the ground too hot for barefoot contact, while increased rainfall can make it too wet and muddy. Extreme weather events, such as hurricanes and heat waves, can also disrupt our ability to connect with the Earth.

On a deeper level, climate change can disrupt the very energy we seek to tap into. The Earth's energy reflects its health, balance, and harmony. As climate change disrupts this balance, it can also disrupt the Earth's energy. This can make it more challenging to achieve the grounding and healing effects of earthing.

However, the challenges posed by climate change also present opportunities. They force us to innovate, adapt, and find new ways of connecting with the Earth. They push us to broaden our understanding of earthing to explore new practices and techniques.

They serve to remind us of the importance of our mission. Earthing is not just about personal wellness; it's about planetary wellness. It's about fostering a deeper connection with the Earth, about nurturing and protecting our planet. As we face the challenges of climate change, we are reminded of our vital role in this mission.

In the face of climate change, earthing takes on a new urgency. It becomes not just a practice but a call to action—a call to reconnect with the Earth, restore its rhythms, and heal its wounds. As we look to the future, we must embrace this call. We must ground ourselves in the Earth, not just for our wellness, but for the wellness of our planet.

Earthing in Urban Landscapes: Challenges and Solutions

In the heart of the city, where concrete and steel dominate the landscape, the concept of earthing may seem like a distant dream. With its relentless pace and artificial structures, the urban environment poses a significant challenge to earthing. Yet, it is precisely in these bustling metropolises where the grounding effects of earthing are most needed.

The primary challenge lies in the need for direct contact with the Earth. High-rise buildings, paved streets, and the scarcity of green spaces create a physical barrier between city dwellers and the Earth's natural energy. The constant exposure to electromagnetic fields from electronic devices and Wi-Fi networks further disrupts our body's natural rhythms, increasing the need for grounding.

However, these challenges are not insurmountable. Innovative solutions are emerging to integrate earthing into urban lifestyles. One such solution is the development of earthing mats and sheets, which mimic the Earth's natural electrical charge and provide a means of grounding even in the city's heart.

Urban planning and architecture are also beginning to acknowledge the importance of earthing. Creating green spaces, rooftop gardens, and incorporating natural elements into building design are all steps towards a more grounded urban lifestyle. These initiatives provide city dwellers with a chance to connect with the Earth and contribute to the overall well-being of the urban environment.

Community initiatives, such as urban gardening and tree planting, also offer opportunities for earthing. These activities bring nature back into the city and foster a sense of community and connection, further enhancing the holistic benefits of earthing.

In the face of these challenges, the future of earthing in urban landscapes looks promising. As awareness grows and solutions evolve, city dwellers will have increasing opportunities to embrace the grounding benefits of earthing. The journey towards a grounded future is not limited to those with access to sprawling landscapes but is a path that can be tread even in the city's heart.

The Role of Earthing in Future Health and Wellness Trends

As we journey deeper into the 21st century, the role of earthing in health and wellness trends is becoming increasingly significant. The world is gradually awakening to the profound benefits of this ancient practice, and its potential to shape our future health landscape is immense.

In the future, we can expect to see earthing integrated into a broader range of health and wellness practices. Already, it is being incorporated into yoga and meditation routines, with practitioners reporting enhanced relaxation and mindfulness. As our understanding of the Earth's energy and its impact on our health continues to grow, we can anticipate a surge in earthing-based therapies and treatments.

Scientific research will likely continually shape the future of earthing in health and wellness trends. As more studies are conducted into the physiological effects of earthing, we can expect to see a greater emphasis on grounding in preventative and curative healthcare. This could range from the use of earthing mats in hospitals to reduce patient recovery times to the promotion of regular grounding exercises as a means of preventing chronic diseases.

In the realm of mental health, earthing holds immense promise. The calming, grounding effect of connecting with the Earth can be a powerful tool in managing stress, anxiety, and depression. As our society grapples with a mental health crisis, earthing could offer a natural, accessible, and cost-effective solution.

The role of earthing in future health and wellness trends is set to be transformative. As we continue to explore and understand the Earth's energy, we will likely see a shift towards more holistic, grounded approaches to health and well-being. By embracing the power of earthing, we can look forward to a future where health is not just about treating illness but about nurturing a deep, sustaining connection with the natural world.

Embracing the Earth's Energy for a Holistic Future

As we draw this exploration of earthing to a close, we find ourselves standing on the precipice of an exciting and uncertain future. The path that lies ahead is not without its challenges but also ripe with potential. It is a future that calls us to embrace the Earth's energy more holistically and meaningfully.

In all its raw and untamed beauty, the Earth has been our constant companion throughout the ages. It has nurtured us, sustained us, and shaped us in ways that are profound and far-reaching. And yet, in our relentless pursuit of progress, we have often overlooked the simple wisdom that the Earth offers. Earthing, as we have come to understand it, is not just a practice or a trend. It is a way of life, a philosophy that invites us to reconnect with the Earth and draw upon its energy to heal, rejuvenate, and thrive.

As we look towards the future, it is clear that earthing will play a pivotal role in shaping our health and wellness trends. The rising popularity of earthing and the advent of technological innovations have opened up new avenues for exploration and growth. From urban landscapes to the farthest corners of the globe, people are beginning to recognize the value of grounding themselves to the Earth.

However, the future of earthing is not without its challenges. Climate change, urbanization, and other global issues pose significant threats to our ability to connect meaningfully with the Earth. However, these challenges also present opportunities for innovation and adaptation. They push us to think creatively and to find new ways of grounding ourselves amidst the chaos and complexity of modern life.

In the end, the future of earthing is in our hands. We must embrace the Earth's energy, integrate it into our daily lives, and pass on this wisdom to future generations. It is a journey that requires courage, commitment, and a deep respect for the Earth and all its wonders.

As we step into this future, remember that earthing is not just about physically grounding ourselves. It is about grounding ourselves emotionally, spiritually, and mentally. It is about finding balance in a world that is often out of balance. It is about embracing the Earth's energy for a holistic future that is not just sustainable but also vibrant, healthy, and deeply connected to the rhythms of the Earth.

Chapter Summary

- The practice of earthing, or grounding, is experiencing a resurgence as people globally seek to reconnect with the Earth's natural energy for its healing and calming effects.
- Despite the challenges posed by modern urban living and the rapid pace of technological innovation, earthing is becoming increasingly popular, with people finding innovative ways to incorporate it into their daily lives.
- Technological advancements, such as grounding mats and earthing shoes, are aiding in making earthing practices more accessible and effective, especially in urban environments.
- Climate change poses a significant challenge to earthing practices, disrupting the Earth's natural rhythms and energy. However, this also presents opportunities for innovation and adaptation in earthing practices.
- Urban landscapes present unique challenges to earthing due to the lack of direct contact with the Earth. However, solutions such as earthing mats, urban planning incorporating green

spaces, and community initiatives make earthing possible in cities.

- Earthing is set to play a significant role in future health and wellness trends, integrating it into yoga, meditation, and potential use in healthcare for preventative and curative purposes.
- The mental health benefits of earthing, including stress and anxiety management, could offer a natural, accessible, and cost-effective solution to the current mental health crisis.
- The future of earthing requires holistically embracing the Earth's energy, integrating it into daily life, and passing on this wisdom to future generations. Despite challenges, earthing presents a path toward a future that is sustainable, vibrant, healthy, and deeply connected to the Earth's rhythms.

10

EARTHING'S CHALLENGES AND CONTROVERSIES

I n alternative health practices, earthing and grounding have sparked much debate. As we delve deeper into the scrutiny and skepticism around earthing, it becomes clear that we must approach the practice with a critical eye.

Some researchers and scientists have argued that much evidence supporting earthing is anecdotal or comes from studies with small sample sizes and methodological limitations. For example, while earlier chapters recounted numerous personal stories of transformation, these compelling narratives carry a different weight than controlled, peer-reviewed research. Concrete evidence must be presented before endorsing any health practice, and earthing is no exception.

Furthermore, the research that exists around earthing is often met with criticism regarding its experimental design. Issues such as lack of proper blinding, inadequate control groups, and potential conflicts of interest are highlighted, particularly when studies are funded by entities with a vested interest in earthing products. These factors can introduce bias and raise concerns about the validity of the findings.

Skeptics point out that the placebo effect could account for many of the positive outcomes reported by individuals while practicing earthing. The placebo effect occurs when a person believes they are receiving a treatment and their symptoms improve despite the treatment having no therapeutic value. This psychological phenomenon is powerful and well-documented, and it can complicate the interpretation of subjective improvements in health.

Another point of contention is the biological plausibility of earthing's purported mechanisms. While it's true that the human body conducts electricity and that the Earth has a mild negative charge due to charged particles from the atmosphere, the leap to specific health benefits is not straightforward. Critics search for a clearer understanding of how this electrical interaction with the body's surface could influence complex physiological processes within the body.

Additionally, the scientific community often calls for a mechanistic explanation consistent with established principles of biology and physics. The body's electrical systems, such as the nervous system and the heart, operate on principles that are well understood, and any claims about earthing must be reconciled with these principles to gain broader acceptance.

Despite these challenges, research on earthing continues, with some studies suggesting potential benefits. However, the scientific community remains cautious until these findings are replicated in larger, more rigorous studies. The skepticism surrounding earthing is a reminder of the importance of maintaining scientific integrity and the need for continued investigation.

As we move forward to the next section, we will explore how the commercialization of earthing products and services has further compli-cated the conversation, raising questions about the integrity of the prac-tice and the motives of those promoting it. It's a world where discernment is critical, and the true essence of earthing must not be lost to the siren call of profit.

Navigating Commercialization and Integrity

In the burgeoning field of earthing, as with any wellness trend that captures the public's imagination, a delicate balance exists between commercial interest and preserving integrity. The promise of reconnecting with the Earth's natural electrical charge has inspired a new movement and spawned a growing product and service industry. This commercialization, while beneficial in spreading awareness and making earthing more accessible, also raises concerns about the dilution of the practice's core principles and the potential for consumer exploitation.

The growth of earthing products such as mats, sheets, and footwear has indeed made it easier for individuals to incorporate grounding into their daily lives, especially for those living in urban environments far away from natural landscapes. Often touted as channels to the Earth's healing energies, these products have been met with enthusiasm and skepticism. While they are a practical solution to modern lifestyle constraints, they are sometimes marketed with claims that stretch beyond the current scientific understanding, raising questions about their true efficacy and value.

As the earthing movement grows, consumers need to navigate this commercial landscape with a critical eye. It's wise to tread carefully and remember that the simplest form of earthing is just a barefoot walk on the ground. The shiny promise of well-marketed earthing products should be weighed against the simplicity of the practice's origins—barefoot contact with the Earth. While some products may offer convenience, they are not always necessary for effective grounding.

The essence of earthing lies in its accessibility and simplicity, and the commercial sector must be careful not to eclipse these virtues with over-priced and overhyped merchandise. Stakeholders within the earthing community must maintain a commitment to transparency, ensuring that products are responsibly marketed and backed by credible research where available.

This is not to suggest that all commercial ventures in the earthing space are inherently misleading. Many businesses are founded by passionate advocates who seek to improve people's health and well-being. These enterprises can play a vital role in supporting scientific research, developing innovative products that genuinely enhance the earthing experience, and educating the public about the benefits of grounding.

However, as with any industry, some may prioritize profit over principle. It is the responsibility of the earthing community—practitioners, researchers, and ethical businesses alike—to uphold standards that ensure the practice remains true to its roots. This includes fostering a culture of integrity where products are sold with honesty about their capabilities and limitations and where the noise of commercial gain does not obscure the primary message.

In conclusion, as earthing continues to captivate hearts and minds around the globe, it is the responsibility of all stakeholders to navigate the waters of commercialization with care and integrity. By putting the well-being of consumers and the Earth first, the earthing movement can flourish in a way that is true to its roots and respectful of the planet it celebrates.

Legal and Regulatory Considerations

As we delve deeper into the complexities surrounding the practice of earthing, it becomes increasingly clear that the path to widespread acceptance is rife with scientific skepticism and legal and regulatory hurdles. These challenges are pivotal in understanding the journey of earthing from a fringe wellness practice to a potentially mainstream health recommendation.

The legal landscape for earthing is as varied as the terrain upon which one might walk barefoot. In the United States, the Food and Drug Administration (FDA) does not currently recognize earthing or grounding as a medical treatment at the time of writing, which means that products related to earthing cannot legally claim to diagnose, treat, cure, or prevent any disease without FDA approval. This presents a significant barrier for those wishing to market earthing products with health claims, as obtaining FDA approval is costly and time-consuming.

The regulatory environment is further complicated because earthing straddles the line between a lifestyle choice and a therapeutic intervention. If earthing products are categorized as medical devices, they would be subject to rigorous scrutiny and must meet specific safety and efficacy standards. However, suppose they are considered wellness or lifestyle products. In that case, they fall into a less stringent regulatory category, which, while easier to navigate, also limits the claims that can be made about their benefits.

The regulatory framework in the European Union (EU) is similarly complex. The EU's Medical Device Regulation (MDR) imposes strict rules on products claiming health benefits. To be legally sold within the EU, earthing products must comply with these regulations, including clinical evaluations and risk assessments. This presents a significant hurdle for earthing proponents seeking to expand their market reach.

Another legal consideration is the patent landscape. As earthing gains popularity, the potential for patent disputes increases. Inventors of earthing-related products may seek patents to protect their innovations, which could lead to legal battles over intellectual property rights. Such disputes can stifle innovation and make it more difficult for new earthing products to enter the market.

Additionally, there is the issue of liability. If an individual were to experience a negative outcome that they attribute to earthing practices or products, the legal considerations could be significant. Manufacturers and advocates should be cautious in how they promote earthing to mitigate the risk of lawsuits stemming from alleged injuries or health issues.

The legal and regulatory hurdles facing earthing are not insurmountable but require careful navigation. Earthing proponents must work within the existing legal framework to responsibly promote their practices and products. This includes conducting the appropriate scientific research to substantiate health claims and ensuring that marketing materials comply with the relevant advertising laws and regulations.

As we transition to the next section, which discusses the integration of earthing into medical practice, it's essential to consider how these legal and regulatory challenges influence the medical community's acceptance and implementation of earthing therapies. The journey of earthing from the ground beneath our feet to the halls of medical institutions is complex, and understanding the legalities involved is a crucial step in that journey.

Earthing and Medical Practice

The concept of earthing has woven its way into the fabric of alternative medicine, allowing individuals to reconnect with the Earth's natural electric charge. Advocates suggest that such a connection can neutralize free radicals, reduce inflammation, and improve overall well-being. However, the integration of earthing into medical practice has been met with interest and skepticism, leading to a complex interplay between anecdotal success stories and the demand for rigorous scientific validation.

On one hand, some healthcare practitioners have embraced earthing as a complementary therapy. These practitioners often draw on the growing body of anecdotal evidence and preliminary scientific studies that suggest a range of health benefits. They argue that earthing offers a non-invasive, natural, and accessible means to potentially enhance patient care. For instance, some nurses have incorporated earthing techniques into patient recovery protocols, reporting improved sleep quality and reduced pain. Similarly, some physicians have recommended earthing mats or pads to patients suffering from chronic inflammatory conditions, noting positive changes in their patients' symptoms.

Despite these encouraging stories, the broader medical community remains cautious. The primary concern is the lack of large-scale, peer-reviewed studies that provide concrete evidence of earthing's efficacy. The medical field, grounded in evidence-based practice, requires rigorous research to substantiate therapeutic claims. Without this, earthing struggles to gain widespread acceptance and remains an outsider to conventional medical treatments.

Critics also point out that the physiological mechanisms proposed by earthing advocates need further investigation. The idea that grounding can influence the body's electrical state and thereby reduce inflammation is intriguing, but the mechanism and extent of these effects still need to be fully understood. This knowledge gap creates a barrier to integrating earthing into standard medical practice, where mechanisms of action are typically well-defined for accepted treatments.

Moreover, there is concern among the medical community about the potential for earthing to be seen as a panacea. There is a risk that individuals may prioritize grounding over established medical treatments, especially in the case of severe health conditions. This concern is compounded by marketing earthing products, which sometimes include bold claims unsupported by substantial scientific evidence.

The individualized nature of health and wellness further complicates the debate over earthing in medical practice. Health is a personal journey; what helps one person might not help another. This variability and the placebo effect make it hard to identify the actual benefits of earthing.

In conclusion, while earthing has found a place within certain corners of healthcare, it remains a subject of debate and scrutiny. The potential for earthing to contribute to patient care is an exciting prospect. Still, more research is necessary to understand its role fully and to establish guidelines for its use in medical practice. With a more robust scientific backing, earthing could one day find its place in healthcare.

Future Earthing Research and Evidence

As we venture into the realm of future research and evidence, it is crucial to acknowledge that the field of earthing and grounding is still in its infancy. Despite the growing body of anecdotal evidence and preliminary studies suggesting many health benefits, earthing remains a contentious topic within the scientific community. The skepticism largely stems from the need for more rigorous, well-designed research studies that can provide concrete evidence to support the claims made by earthing proponents.

The future of earthing research lies at a critical crossroads. To move beyond the challenges and controversies, researchers must embark on a path that adheres to the gold standards of scientific inquiry. This could involve conducting randomized controlled trials with larger sample sizes to test the effects of earthing on various health outcomes.

One of the critical areas for future exploration is the impact of earthing on inflammation. Inflammation is a common thread linking many chronic diseases, and earthing's potential anti-inflammatory effects are a central pillar of its proposed health benefits. Researchers must seek to quantify these effects and understand the pathways through which grounding may influence the body's inflammatory response. They need to measure, understand, and see it in action across different groups of people to make progress truly.

Another avenue for research is the exploration of earthing's effects on sleep and circadian rhythms. Sleep disorders and disturbances are rampant in modern society, and preliminary evidence suggests that grounding may improve sleep quality and normalize circadian rhythms.

The cardiovascular system is another area ripe for investigation. Early studies have indicated that earthing may influence blood flow, blood pressure, and heart rate variability. To build on these findings, researchers could conduct long-term studies to assess whether regular earthing practices can contribute to cardiovascular health and potentially reduce the risk of heart disease.

The psychological effects of earthing are an intriguing subject for future research. While personal stories have highlighted improvements in stress levels, mood, and overall well-being, empirical evidence is needed to substantiate these claims. Standardized assessments could paint a clearer picture of the psychological benefits of grounding and its impact on parameters such as stress, anxiety, and depression.

In addition to these specific health outcomes, future research could also address the practical aspects of earthing. How often should we earth, and for how long? Are all these products necessary, or can we get by with just the ground beneath our feet?

It is also essential for future studies to consider the potential placebo effect, which could contribute to the perceived benefits of earthing. By incorporating sham grounding as a control condition, researchers can better determine the actual effects of earthing.

Finally, as we look to the future, research in earthing must be conducted with transparency and a commitment to open science. By sharing data and methodologies, researchers can facilitate better studies and contribute to a more robust and credible evidence base. Only through collaboration and transparency can we overcome the challenges and controversies surrounding earthing and pave the way for a clearer understanding of its place in health and wellness.

Chapter Summary

- Earthing's empirical support is often anecdotal or from small, methodologically flawed studies, lacking the weight of controlled, peer-reviewed research.
- Positive outcomes from earthing could also be attributed to the placebo effect, where belief in treatment leads to perceived health improvements without therapeutic action.
- Existing earthing studies face criticism for issues like lack of blinding, inadequate control groups, and potential conflicts of interest, especially when earthing product entities fund such studies.
- Critics seek a clearer explanation of how earthing's electrical interactions with the body's surface could affect complex internal physiological processes.
- Claims about earthing must align with established biological and physical principles, particularly regarding the body's electrical systems.
- Despite making earthing more accessible, the commercialization of earthing products raises concerns about the dilution of earthing's core principles and potential consumer exploitation.
- Earthing faces challenges with FDA recognition and EU regulations, affecting how products can be marketed and the claims they can make.
- While some healthcare practitioners use earthing as a complementary therapy, the broader medical community requires more substantial evidence for widespread acceptance.
- Future research could focus on rigorous, well-designed studies exploring earthing's effects on inflammation, sleep, circadian rhythms, cardiovascular health, and psychological well-being while accounting for the placebo effect.

EMBRACING THE EARTH'S EMBRACE

As we draw the curtain on this exploration of earthing, it is fitting to revisit our journey together. We embarked on this path with a simple premise: that the Earth beneath our feet, often taken for granted, holds a profound potential for healing and connection. We sought to understand the concept of earthing, delve into its roots, explore its branches, and see how it intertwines with our lives and well-being.

Our journey began with the basic understanding of earthing as a practice of grounding oneself to the Earth, of making direct contact with its surface. We explored the science behind this practice, the flow of electrons from the Earth into our bodies, and the potential benefits this exchange could bring. We delved into the history of our relationship with the Earth, tracing back to our ancestors who lived in harmony with nature, their feet firmly planted on the ground.

We then ventured into the heart of earthing, exploring how it can be integrated into our daily lives and the experiences of those who have embraced this practice. We heard stories of healing, transformation, and a renewed sense of connection to the Earth and oneself. We saw how earthing could serve as a bridge, linking the physical and the spiritual, the individual and the collective, the human and the Earth.

Throughout this journey, we have also grappled with the challenges and critiques of earthing. We have acknowledged the limitations of our current understanding, the gaps in our knowledge, and the need for further research. We have wrestled with the practicalities of earthing in our modern, urbanized world and the potential barriers to its widespread adoption.

As we stand at the end of this journey, we are not the same as when we began. We have unearthed a deeper understanding of earthing, its potential, and its challenges. We have seen the Earth not just as a passive surface beneath our feet but as an active participant in our lives, a source of healing and connection. We have felt the Earth's embrace, and in doing so, we have come to see ourselves and our place in the world in a new light.

In the following sections, we will delve deeper into our journey's major themes and findings, the implications and significance of earthing, and the limitations and critiques we have encountered. We will conclude with some final thoughts and recommendations as we look to the future of our relationship with the Earth.

Unearthing the Core Insights

In this section, we delve into the heartwood of our exploration, unearthing the core insights that have emerged from our journey into the realm of earthing. These themes and findings, like the roots of a mighty oak, reach deep into the soil of our understanding, anchoring our knowledge and nourishing our perspective.

Interconnectedness

The first central theme surfacing is the profound interconnectedness of all life. Earthing is not an isolated practice but a manifestation of the intricate web of relationships that bind us to the Earth and each other. When we ground ourselves, we connect with the Earth's surface and the myriad forms of life that share our planetary home. This realization brings a sense of humility, a recognition of our place within the grand tapestry of existence.

Transformative Power of Earthing

The second theme is the transformative power of earthing. Throughout our exploration, we have seen how this simple act can profoundly change physical health, emotional well-being, and spiritual awareness. From reducing inflammation and improving sleep to fostering a sense of calm and enhancing our connection with the natural world, the benefits of earthing are as diverse as they are significant.

Accessibility

The third theme is the accessibility of earthing. Unlike many wellness practices, earthing does not require expensive equipment or specialized knowledge. It is a practice available to all, regardless of age, fitness level, or socioeconomic status. This democratization of wellness is a powerful reminder that the most effective healing practices are often the simplest and most natural.

Resilience

Finally, we have discovered the theme of resilience. Earthing, we have found, is not just about grounding in the present moment but also about cultivating the strength and flexibility to weather life's storms. By connecting with the Earth, we tap into a source of stability and vitality that can sustain us through times of stress and change.

$\sim$

These themes, while distinct, are deeply interwoven. They tell a story of connection, transformation, accessibility, and resilience—a story that is not just about earthing but about our relationship with the Earth and with ourselves. As we move forward, let us keep these insights close to our hearts, allowing them to guide us on our continued journey into the embrace of the Earth.

Implications and Significance: The Ripple Effect of Grounding

As we delve into the third section of our concluding chapter, we find ourselves standing at the edge of a vast, interconnected web of implications and significance. This is where we begin to truly comprehend the ripple effect of grounding, the profound impact that earthing has on our lives and the world around us.

The act of grounding and physically connecting ourselves to the Earth is not merely a solitary act of self-care. It is a gesture of unity, a silent acknowledgment of our shared existence with the natural world. Each time we ground ourselves, we send out ripples of energy, vibrations that echo through the fabric of our lives and those around us.

The implications of grounding are manifold. On a personal level, grounding has been shown to promote physical and emotional well-being. It helps to reduce stress, improve sleep, and enhance overall vitality. It is a simple, accessible practice that can be incorporated into our daily routines, a gentle reminder of our inherent connection to the Earth.

On a broader scale, grounding fosters a sense of environmental stewardship. It reminds us of our responsibility to care for the Earth, to protect and preserve the natural world for future generations. It encourages us to live in harmony with nature and respect our ecosystem's delicate balance.

The significance of grounding extends even further, reaching into spirituality and philosophy. Grounding is a tangible expression of our interconnectedness, a physical manifestation of the spiritual concept that we are all one. It challenges us to reconsider our place in the universe and to question the artificial boundaries that separate us from the natural world.

However, grounding has its critiques and limitations, which we have explored. Despite these challenges, the practice of grounding holds immense potential. It offers a path towards greater health, harmony, and understanding, a way to nurture our bond with the Earth.

As we move forward, let us consider these implications and significance. Let us remember the ripple effect of grounding, the profound impact our actions can have on ourselves, our communities, and our world. Let us embrace the Earth's embrace, grounding ourselves in the knowledge that we are all part of the same beautiful, intricate web of life.

Limitations and Critiques: The Unpaved Path of Earthing

As we tread further into the heart of this chapter, it is essential to acknowledge that the path of earthing, like any other, has its rough patches. The unpaved earthing path is strewn with limitations and critiques that we must address with an open mind and a willing spirit.

The first limitation we encountered was the need for more extensive scientific research on earthing. While preliminary studies have shown promising results, the field is still in its infancy. The effects of grounding on human health still need to be fully understood, and the mechanisms through which these effects occur remain primarily speculative. This lack of empirical evidence can make it challenging to convince skeptics of the benefits of earthing, and it also leaves room for misinterpretation and misinformation.

Another critique often leveled at earthing is its perceived impracticality. In our modern, urbanized world, many live in high-rise buildings and work in office environments where direct contact with the Earth is not always feasible. Critics argue that earthing is a luxury only those with access to natural environments can afford. However, this critique overlooks the various simple grounding techniques and tools used indoors, such as grounding mats and sheets.

The unpaved path of earthing also faces the challenge of commercialization. As earthing gains popularity, there is a risk that profit-driven motives could dilute its essence. The market is already flooded with many grounding products, some of which make exaggerated claims without substantial evidence. This commercialization can lead to skepticism and cynicism, potentially overshadowing the genuine benefits of earthing.

Lastly, there is a critique that earthing oversimplifies the complex nature of human health. Critics argue that grounding may contribute to well-being but is not a panacea for all health issues. It is crucial to remember that earthing is a complementary practice, not a substitute for professional medical advice and treatment.

Despite these limitations and critiques, the earthing path holds immense potential. It invites us to reconnect with our natural environment, listen to the subtle rhythms of the Earth, and rediscover nature's healing power. As we navigate this path, let us do so with humility, curiosity, and a deep respect for the Earth's wisdom.

Nurturing the Bond with Earth

On this journey, we have delved into the heart of the Earth, felt its pulse beneath our bare feet, and discovered the profound impact it can have on our physical and emotional well-being.

In nurturing our bond with the Earth, we are not merely engaging in a passive act of connection. Instead, we actively participate in a symbiotic relationship, a dance of energy exchange as old as life. The Earth gives us life and sustains us, and in return, we must care for it, respect it, and honor its rhythms.

The practice of earthing is not a panacea for all ailments nor a substitute for medical treatment. However, it is a powerful tool in our wellness toolkit, a natural remedy that can complement and enhance our overall health and well-being. It is a gentle reminder of our inherent connection to the natural world, a connection that is often overlooked in our fast-paced, technology-driven lives.

As we move forward, I hope you continue exploring and deepening your relationship with the Earth. Make it a daily practice to walk barefoot on the grass, feel the Earth beneath your feet, and listen to its whispers in the rustling leaves and the murmuring streams. Allow yourself to be grounded, held, and nurtured by the Earth's embrace.

Remember, earthing is not a destination but a journey. It is a path of discovery, self-awareness, healing, and growth. It is a path that leads us back to our roots, true nature, and essence of who we are.

In conclusion, I invite you to embrace the Earth's embrace. Feel its energy, vitality, and life force flowing through you. To recognize and honor the sacred bond that exists between you and the Earth. To nurture this bond, cherish it, and let it guide you toward health, happiness, and holistic well-being.

May the Earth's embrace be your grounding force, healing balm, and constant companion on this beautiful journey we call life.

EPILOGUE

As our journey through the heart of nature's realm draws to a close, let us take a moment to breathe—to let the essence of the forest and the soul of the earth linger within us. "Grounded in Nature" has been a vessel, carrying us across the gentle streams of wisdom and through the lush groves of understanding.

In the quiet afterglow of our exploration, may you carry the whispers of the leaves in your heart and the grounding touch of the Earth in your spirit. As you return to the world beyond these pages, remember that the canopy of leaves, the rustle of grass, and the caress of the wind are ever-present companions on your journey through life. They wait patiently, ready to welcome you back into their healing embrace.

May the seeds planted within this book flourish within you, growing into a life lived with deeper connection, vibrant health, and a soul nourished by the timeless rhythm of nature. Go forth with eyes open to the beauty surrounding you, with feet eager to tread upon the Earth, and with a heart full of the serene power you have rediscovered here.

And so, dear reader, as you close this book, do not see it as an ending but as the beginning of a newfound relationship with the world outside your door. Let every step upon the Earth be a note in the symphony of your life and every breath of forest air a brushstroke on the canvas of your days. Be forever grounded in nature, and in doing so, be forever at home.

ABOUT THE AUTHOR

Naomi Rohan is a devoted author and expert in natural wellness. With a deep-rooted passion for holistic health, she has dedicated her life to exploring and sharing the healing power of nature. Her books, which delve into topics such as forest bathing and earthing, have become essential reading for those seeking to reconnect with the natural world for their well-being.

Naomi's journey began with a degree in the field of natural sciences, which laid the foundation for her understanding of the intricate relationship between humans and nature. She further honed her knowledge through extensive travels, immersing herself in diverse cultures and their unique healing practices.

Naomi's work is characterized by her vivid, expressive writing style and ability to translate complex concepts into accessible, practical advice. She has a unique knack for guiding her readers on a journey of self-discovery and healing, helping them to find balance and harmony in their lives.

When she's not writing, Naomi can be found wandering in the woods, barefoot on the beach, or tending to her herb garden. She continues to be a student of nature, constantly learning, evolving, and sharing her wisdom with the world.

FREE EBOOK BY NAOMI ROHAN: Nurtured by Nature

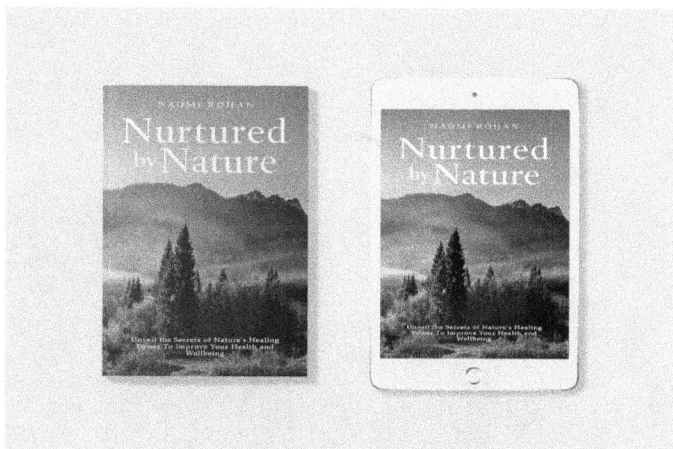

$9.99 FREE EBOOK

Scan the QR code below to download your free copy of Nurtured by Nature:

Or visit:
https://teilingenpress.wixsite.com/home/naomi-rohan